FARM MEMORIES

An Illustrated History of Rural Life

April Halberstadt

Motorbooks International
Publishers & Wholesalers ®

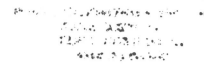

First published in 1996 by Motorbooks International Publishers & Wholesalers, 729 Prospect Avenue, PO Box 1, Osceola, WI 54020-0001 USA

Motorbooks International books are also available at discounts in bulk quantity for industrial or sales-promotional use. For details write to Special Sales Manager at the Publisher's address

Library of Congress Cataloging-in-Publication Data available

ISBN 0-7603-0161-1

Printed in the United States of America

CONTENTS

Dedication

For my children

Bronwyn Anne Johnston

and Christopher Quentin Johnston.

They are the first generation away from

Mount Ayr, Iowa, and Bean Lake, Missouri.

Acknowledgments

During the last few years, my husband, Hans, and I have been traveling around the farm areas of America. We have photographed and researched the history and operation of various types of farm equipment for several book projects. It's always a thrilling experience to see and hear those enormous early steam engines and threshers, still functional and operating, but relegated mostly to living-history museums and private collections. Thousands of American tractors are also operational, still too good to throw away, but without any real work to do. It is fascinating to look at these complex and sophisticated pieces of machinery and see how quickly technology has changed farm life. It has made me think about how much farms have changed since I was a child.

As we have traveled around, looking at all this equipment has provoked more questions about farm technology and agricultural history than we can find answers for. A lot of facts about farming, the stuff that "everybody knows," seems to have been ignored, forgotten, or mislaid. Understanding the improvements in technology was easy because the farm equipment almost spoke for itself. But we frequently found ourselves asking, I wonder why they did it that way? because the reason for a custom or procedure is no longer obvious.

We found some oral histories about farm customs and practices, but we realized that important information was missing. Some information about everyday life, certain sanitary practices, for example, was missing because no one talked about it in public. Writing about it was probably considered extremely rude and vulgar. We find fleeting references, such as the line we came across about "sewing Pop into his union suit when the weather turned cold." The reader is then left to presume that (a) the old man never bathed, or (b) the old man bathed with his underwear on, or (c) he never needed to bathe in the winter. Was this a common custom? we asked ourselves.

At the other extreme, some answers were missing because the common customs were once so obvious that no explanations were needed. For example, we recalled that a shower bath was unheard of on the farm even in my time, unless you got caught in the rain. My children were a little incredulous—no showers? It took some recollecting to remember that a farmer would never let precious water just pour down a drain. The dishwater was recycled, the wash water used more than once, and boiling water was poured over dishes stacked in a rinse basin. A shower would be considered wasteful.

So I have frequently had to call on the rural recollections and insights of my dad, John Hope, or his good friend Orrin Long. Orrin farms near Valley Falls, Kansas, and shares his experiences and optimistic observations on the future of farming. I have consulted a number of other relatives and acquaintances who have been tolerant and amused but always forthcoming. These include Agnes Bird in Grants Pass, Oregon, and her brother-in-law, William Bird, among others. Mr. Bird is a writer and retired editor of *The Country Gentleman* magazine and he lives in Philadelphia.

I have called on my favorite veterinarian, my sister, Esther Hope, DVM, to answer questions like, "What is the 'mad itch,' and is it still a farm problem?" And Patrick Clark at the James Jerome Hill reference library in St. Paul, Minnesota, has cheerfully answered even stranger queries.

Dozens of others have contributed directly or indirectly to this memoir; many of them are mentioned in the stories that follow, and we thank them all for straightening us out on how things really were. And while I am mentioning special contributions, I should also single out Zack Miller, the editor at Motorbooks International who germinated this idea, and of course the rest of the staff in Osceola, Wisconsin, who have variously cultivated and pruned this product to bring it to market—so to speak.

$\mathscr{P}$reface

$\mathscr{I}$ was born and raised in Kansas City, Missouri, the origin of the Santa Fe Trail and the Oregon Trail and the Gateway to the Great Plains. The farms in my life belonged to my grandparents and their neighbors. My paternal grandparents owned a 68-acre farm near Pleasant Hill, Missouri. My other grandparents owned a very rural retreat, an old one-room schoolhouse on 89 acres near Hermitage in the Missouri Ozarks. My experiences of country life come from childhood visits with the neighbors and friends in both communities.

I have to admit that while I didn't mind feeding the chickens, I never volunteered for cleaning them (ugh). Milking cows was tolerable but a short-lived experience for me; lessons were suspended after grandma's Jersey kicked her one morning. I will also confess that my interest in farm life was superficial and probably pretty transparent; I was lobbying for a horse. Horses, cows, sheep, and hogs; corn and

A bumper crop of corn in the crib, this hard-working family displays the fruit of a year of labor. *Halbe Collection, The Kansas State Historical Society*

How I envy Miss Sadie Austin, described as a typical Nebraska cowgirl from Cherry County, standing with her guns and her horse around 1900. I wanted to be a cowgirl with a real horse. It's hard to tell whether Miss Austin is actually authentic in her imitation buckskins made of polished cotton and with an old Colt tucked in her belt. But the shotgun looks real and the horse looks impatient, so maybe Miss Sadie is not merely posing. *Solomon D. Butcher Collection, Nebraska State Historical Society*

wheat . . . in the middle of it all, I was always aware that Kansas City, the heart of America, was the center of the American agricultural universe, too.

Growing up in the Midwest meant listening to the daily market reports on the radio in the morning before school. The current prices of wheat, corn, and sow bellies were on WHB radio at 6 A.M., along with the weather and other important farm information. Since Kansas City was a market town, it meant seeing the daily truckloads of cattle and squealing hogs being hauled to the 'yards in the "bottoms," as we walked to school in the morning. You tried not to get too close, especially when the trucks were stopped at traffic lights.

Oats cut and bound the old-fashioned way, awaiting pick up.

A larger-than-life white-faced steer marked the offices of the American Hereford Association on the bluffs overlooking the Kansas City stockyards. And every November we looked forward to a major event, the American Royal Parade and Horse Show. The Future Farmers of America (FFA) usually held its convention at the same time. Kansas City streets were filled with young men in dark blue corduroy jackets and wide-brimmed hats, coming to town from Chillicothe and Cameron, Missouri; from Des Moines and Dubuque, Iowa; from Hays and Hutchinson, Kansas.

Going away to school later on introduced me to new friends, many of whom grew up on farms.

One roommate had worked every summer detasseling corn, another was a prestigious festival princess. Classmates had earned school money bucking hay or picking hops.

Well, it's almost all gone now. The American Royal is still an important event, but the number of heads of livestock rolling into Kansas City stockyards is now much smaller. The grain elevators, the packing plants, the feed and seed distributors, the mills and the agricultural equipment distributors have mostly disappeared. I find all of the vacant buildings in the West Bottoms of Kansas City to be disquieting.

When I started doing the research for the book projects my husband and I had undertaken, looking at historic material in museums and libraries, I noticed that farm technology has always changed very quickly in America. So my uneasiness about the apparent speed of change on the farm has been replaced by a fascination with the progressive mindset of the American farmer.

My old economics textbook said that you needed four things to start a business: land, labor, capital, and an entrepreneur. I can see now that it was the American farmer who first brought it all together for us. It's the farmer who was the first capitalist, who made America a nation of entrepreneurs. And it's the farmer who continues to use and adapt all sorts of technology years before it shows up for everyday use by the average suburban consumer.

I realized that I had met farmers using car phones back in 1962. Farmers used airplanes for seeding and spraying before World War II, and they used satellite dishes and CB radios as soon as they came on the market. Most farmers consider in vitro fertilization, recombinant DNA, and embryo transfer old news. The cover of a recent issue of *Farm Journal* mag-

We cherish our farm memories. This old truck belongs to the Peltzer family and was once used to haul water. Now it sits in the shed, too tired to work but still loved.

azine shows an Indiana farmer using a spraying rig that is guided by a satellite navigation system.

This book offers a chance to look at how we were, and think about where we are now. And then consider how we got here. It's a chance to compare our views with the information found in the old farming magazines, just to see how much difference all those new-fangled machines really made.

This book pulls together some of our observations and discoveries from various people, old farm magazines, old agricultural textbooks, and several state historical society archives around agricultural America. We even put in a few of the old jokes. After all, rural Americans cultivated corny humor.

You are invited to look at some old pictures, read some old advertisements, listen to a few of the folks we talked with and enjoy the ramble.

Introduction

$\mathcal{W}$hen you think about it, American farmers produced an entirely new way of developing a nation's economy. Our early immigrant farmers came from Europe, where wealth was tied to systems of inheritance and feudal boundaries. If you were lucky, you farmed land inherited from your father. If you weren't lucky, you farmed for someone else. Nobody made a fortune from their farm.

As the number of family farms in America gets smaller, the misconceptions about farm life seem to become greater. Bryan Jones put his thoughts down in an amusing and fascinating book called *The Farming Game,* and his chapter on "The Last Capitalist" is especially thought-provoking. He reminds us that, first and foremost, farming is about making money. It's not a lifestyle and it's not a tax

Although the Homestead Act was first signed in 1862, rural families such as the Yankoski family were still taking advantage of homestead benefits in Beltrami Island, Minnesota, nearly 75 years later. And while many rural students were riding a school bus by 1936 when this picture was taken, the Yankoski children are going to school via a more traditional type of transportation.
Paul Carter photo, Library of Congress, FSA

shelter. It's not a hobby. People go into business—the farm business and every other business—to make money.

Farming used to be extremely hard labor for both a man and his wife. If you were a farmer, you were usually poor. Respectable, but poor. Farming was an honorable occupation, unlike some of the more questionable work found in town. Many farmers especially valued the opportunity "to be their own man" and not take orders from a landlord. But by and large, even though their independence was respected, farmers were mostly uneducated and considered to be a lower class.

Jones reminds us that America, the land that started as a nation of immigrant farmers, quickly became a nation of capitalists and entrepreneurs. The American government made it possible for residents to acquire land through the Homestead Act of 1862. Successful homesteaders then moved from a farm to farm-related businesses. Farmers frequently mortgaged their crop to buy a mowing machine or a thresher. Then they could acquire extra income by custom threshing. Sometimes the weather turned bad and they lost the crop, the new thresher, and their farm. But sometimes they did well, bought the next farm, or started a related agricultural business such as a grain elevator, a feed store, or an equipment dealership.

Farm prosperity in the Old World had been tied mostly to providence. The farmer had a good year if the weather held, pestilence was minimal, and the army from a neighboring country was quiet. But hard winters or drought frequently brought widespread famine. Everyone knew that a summer hailstorm or the neighbor's livestock could destroy a crop in an afternoon. War and political unrest were beyond providence, however,

One man, one farm. This picture recalls the corny joke that "here is a fellow out standing in his field." *Ritzville Public Library*

11

This rare push mower is a collector's item today. This early mower allowed the farmer to keep an eye on both his team of mules and his machine, making a one-man harvesting operation possible. *Halbe Collection, The Kansas State Historical Society*

and such man-made turmoil forced many farmers to move; farmers have always had to keep one eye on the politicians.

When European farmers looked elsewhere for opportunity their eyes fell on America, the land of opportunity and the place to get rich. It was a land where you could acquire as large a farm as you could manage—hundreds of acres if you wanted them. It was a country without centuries of warfare, a place where farmers only had to worry about the weather.

The Disappearing Farmer

Consider some numbers from the Census Bureau that often accompany articles about the disappearing family farm. At face value, the numbers might seem disturbing. But since Americans seem to be eating pretty well—much too well, according to some

One farmer and one team, plowing, planting, cultivating, harvesting.

sources—the numbers need some thoughtful interpretation.

Looking at 150 years of American agriculture, it's clear that we have moved from being a rural nation to an urban one. But despite increasing population, we have increased both productivity and the numbers of farm products.

Are we really being fed by less than 2 percent of the population? Well, the 2-percenters

Census Year	U.S. Population	Farm Residents	% Workers[2]
1850	23,191,876	11,680,000[1]	64
1900	75,994,575	29,414,000[1]	38
1950	150,697,361	25,058,000	11
1990	248,710,000	4,591,000	1.9

[1] *Estimated by the Census Bureau.*

[2] *Percent engaged in farm labor. This column of percentages is not the product of the numbers in the other two columns. This is how the Census Bureau counts it.*

Education has always been an important component of American frontier life. Local schools were established even before churches and other community buildings. *Halbe Collection, The Kansas State Historical Society*

Now don't you feel sorry for all those poor kids in town who never have any fun? Spring is here, the irises are up, and this happy, young Jayhawker from western Kansas is wearing his new costume and practicing for a show. *Halbe Collection, The Kansas State Historical Society*

have a lot of support from farm-related industries that are not now being defined as farm workers. To my mind, the United States Census shows how efficient and productive the American farmer has become. But all of those other farm-production people who support the

farmer are no longer being counted as farm workers because they no longer have an address on the old rural route.

Farm workers still make jelly, pack pickles, and process vegetables. But now it's a commercial co-op that does the food preparation and butchering that used to be done on the farm. A farm wife has a choice of baking bread and making butter or picking it up at a grocery, but given the reduced prices of some commodities, it now costs more for her to do it at home.

Nonetheless, the numbers seem to us to validate a trend, the perception that we are moving away from farm land and farm life. We find this trend disquieting. Perhaps we mourn the loss of our farm culture, one important foundation under the American national experience. In less than two centuries we built a wealthy nation upon some new attitudes about farming and independence. Perhaps we fear that when our farms disappear, the values, attitudes, and independent spirit that underlie our national strength and success will disappear, too. As farmer Orrin Long has observed, "Nature is an honest world, a dependable world, and we need this sort of world in order to maintain our spirit." So we try hanging on to what we can, bits and pieces of old farm crockery or equipment or tools, finding comfort in our farm memories.

CHAPTER ONE

Types of Farms

All Farms Are Not Created Equal

If you grew up in a Midwestern farming community, you know that there is a sort of class system among farmers. There are some kinds of farming that are well, uh . . . more respected than others. And while the Department of Agriculture may group all farmers into a single occupational class, there are some very distinct differences within the occupation.

"Real" farmers raise wheat or corn or row crops. Or they feed cattle. Or they do both. Row-crop farming includes vegetables and some fruits. And while orchardists are certainly considered farmers, Christmas tree growers . . . well, that's a sideline, not a crop. Hothouse farming is a real specialty; growing tomatoes and flowers for the winter months in glass-covered warehouses can be very profitable. But out in California, they'll raise anything and call it farming.

Families like this opened the Great Plains for farming. Mother and the girls have come to the field to see how Father and the boys are faring with the mowing and binding. Farming was a family affair with every member making an effort. Though the drudgery compelled many youngsters to vow that they would leave the farm as soon as possible, some, such as Henry Ford, would remember their roots and try to ease the farmer's burden through mechanical assistance. *Halbe Collection, The Kansas State Historical Society*

Cattle Ranch near Deer Creek, Nebraska, circa 1900. The sand hills of central Nebraska could be dry and desolate but you'd never know it to look at these fat and healthy cattle. *Solomon D. Butcher Collection, Nebraska State Historical Society*

There is also a big difference between farming and ranching, although there are some obvious similarities. Ranching produces cattle and sheep, mostly on the open range. Dairies obviously employ cows as well, but they are called farms rather than ranches, and "feeding" cattle rather than letting them forage for themselves makes a beef operation a farm rather than a ranch. Don't get the two confused. You really have to watch yourself out there in western Kansas or Oklahoma. You might just say something so dumb that local folks will talk about you for years.

Farming is about making money and the dilettante is not really respected, but that is true whether the occupation is farming or insurance sales. The

Improved roads and creamery co-ops helped the dairy farmer. Cans of milk from local farmers being unloaded at the creamery in Coleraine, Minnesota, during the late 1930s. *John Vachon photo, Library of Congress, FSA*

successful salesman, however, generally looks pretty prosperous while many of the richest, most successful farmers wear the same ratty baseball cap they received from their implement dealer when they took delivery on their combine two years ago. So it's frequently difficult for an outsider to tell who has the best operation in the area.

On our road there were three real farmers: one had a small dairy operation, one practiced mixed farming, and one raised corn and beans. Three other families on our road were retired farmers, like my grandparents. Retirement usually meant that while they lived in the farmhouse, their fields were plowed and planted by someone else for a share of the harvest. But even if you were retired you still had chores to do every day.

There was one family that we never associated with, other than to give a friendly wave as we passed their house on our way to the highway. They were new people who had moved a mobile home onto their acreage and then brought in a few sheep to graze the weeds down. I

Bud Hicks, he was a simple lad,
Who never done no harm.
He milked a cow from the left-hand side,
And now he's left the farm!

The Country Gentleman, 1918.

had the impression that they were not considered real farmers, just folks who would be moving on. "Nice folks . . .," we'd say, waving as we drove past. "Works over in town," my grandmother would observe dryly.

There were several other rural operations that were not considered real farming in the part of the country where I grew up. One was raising horses—quarter horses or trotters. This was seen as a hobby for the independently wealthy, someone with enough spare time to go around to the various horse shows. Then there were the experimenters, farm folks who were always going to make big money by trying something new. Raising chinchillas for fur coats was a big industry for a while; mink farming was also very common when ownership of a "ranch mink" coat was a sign of prosperity. Ostrich farming—or is it called ranching?—seems to be undergoing another wave of popularity. Squab, angora goats, and merino sheep all have had their devotees and their places in the market over the years.

How We Got 21 Tons of Pork from 20 Brood Sows

Then there are hogs. Hog farmers are in a group by themselves, and that is usually the way they like it. A farmer who raises hogs usually raises only hogs and maybe the corn to feed them, nothing else. Hogs have no sweat glands so they need water or mud to regulate their body temperature. Their sharp hooves and their manure can ruin a pasture for other types of crops, and they stink like few other farm animals. On the other side of the ledger, hogs are extremely profitable and all the early farm magazines have articles about "Raising a Ton of Pork." This article from

the January 1927 issue of *Farm and Fireside* was written by Harry Christensen, a hog farmer from Webster City, Iowa:

Last year we raised 223 pigs from the first 20 sows that farrowed. They went to market in 180 days, averaging 191 pounds each, or 2,100 pounds to the litter.

When I got back from flying in the army I wasn't interested in hogs. I wanted to do something with a lot of action, like high-pressure grain and tractor farming. But my brother, who is county agent here in Hamilton County, and my partner held out for hogs. I could raise all the corn I wanted to, he said, but it ought to be marketed as meat.

It paid very well. Our records show we paid $4,335.66 for feed including 10 acres of alfalfa pasture. Most of the corn cost 95 cents a bushel. The hogs brought $8,200, leaving a profit of more than $3,800.

It was possible to produce 2,000 pounds of marketable meat in one year from one litter of piglets, and prices have improved with better production techniques. So don't call them piggies; those are what go in your booties. Say "swine" if you want to be taken seriously.

Dairy Farming—How to Keep the Girls Happy

Dairy farms are special and so are dairy farmers. Sometimes you see other farmers shake their heads in amazement at both the amount of work and the amount of money in dairy farming. First of all, it's a 365-days-a-year proposition: the girls always need attention. Because of the special relationship between the farmer and his herd, dairy farming may be something of a vocation—you have to be called to do it.

The dairy industry was one of the first agribusinesses to carefully record and market genetic heritage. This is Hardwick's King Masher, specially groomed for photographer H. A. Stohmeyer in 1928. Stohmeyer's studio was in New York and he promoted himself as "Photographer of Animals." With thousands of dollars at stake, hiring a specialist to promote a prize bull was a good investment.

"Valley of the Heart's Delight" was the name given to the glorious vista of the prune and apricot orchards in Santa Clara Valley. Tourists came to see the spring blossoms until the mid-1960s. Today the orchards have all been replaced by the electronics industry manufacturers of Silicon Valley. *San Jose Historical Museum*

An interview with Bob Shuford of Catawba County, North Carolina, in a *Farm and Fireside* story from January 1927 is probably a pretty typical description of older dairy farmers: "I've had 33 years of dairy farming, and I still find it fascinating. And I believe that when my boy is as old as I am, he will feel the same way about it." Shuford farmed near Newton and started with 50 acres. When he was interviewed, he had 500 acres whose worth he estimated, together with his farm ice-cream factory, at about $100,000.

But while large-scale dairy operations have been part of American farm industry for a century, most of

The Country Gentleman, 1918.

the small farms used to keep a cow, too. And milking the cow used to be women's work during my grandmother's lifetime; none of her cows was ever milked by machine. Although milking machines were not new, only one farmer, the small dairy operator on our road, had them. And we surmised that the reason he had the machines was that his four children were all very young, and his wife was obviously so busy that she could not help with chores. So he was forced to milk with machines. This revelation was invariably concluded with the remark that "the cows don't seem to mind."

Milking a Cow

Milking is done twice a day. The milkmaid washes her hands and gathers up her sanitized bucket, her stool, and a clean cloth and heads out into the pasture to find the cow. If the cow is uncomfortable because she is full of milk, she will be complaining, so she is not too hard to find.

Tie the cow's halter to a nearby tree or fence, squat comfortably on the stool and clench the milk bucket between your knees. The cow has four teats and the milk has to be stripped from each one, a process that may take about 20 minutes if you are a practiced milker. Grab a teat in each

The Country Gentleman, 1915.

hand, squeeze firmly while pulling gently down, alternating your hands. Squeeze and pull left, squeeze and pull right, squeeze and pull left . . . you should get a nice little rhythm going, the milk singing as it hits the bucket. There is a little knack to it, but like driving a tractor or riding a horse, it's easy once you've done it.

That was the easy part. Now for the hard part: while you are sitting there tugging away, the cow is moving around, chewing on food, stamping her feet, swishing her tail, and pooping. You want to stay away from all of these activities, and it's hard to do. You are bent over, hanging on to your bucket with your knees because she has been known to kick it over.

Sometimes the cow kicks the bucket over because she's just being a clumsy old cow. But sometimes she's annoyed at you and she will kick you on purpose. Cows have feelings, too.

When one teat starts to run dry, grab another one until all four are done. You are doing this mostly by feel since your forehead is dug into the cow's side. If your hands are too cold or too rough, she'll let you know.

Cultivating in one of Santa Clara County, California's many orchards was hazardous to both horse and driver as well as to the trees. Limbs were easily broken, leaving trees vulnerable to disease . . . and you could probably say the same about the farmer and his horse. The development of specialized orchard equipment would help. *San Jose Historical Museum*

Move your bucket out of the way in a hurry when you are finished. Put the clean cloth over the top to keep flies and other dirt out of your heavy bucket as you try to haul it back across the pasture to the cooler without spilling it. The milking operation and its related mishaps have contributed two important philosophical sayings to American life: "There's no use crying over spilt milk" and "Well, he finally kicked the bucket."

This was the usual procedure in the olden days, when there was one cow and one milkmaid and they were on familiar terms with each other. Nowadays it's more difficult to really get to know a cow so it's safer to bring the cow into a milking station.

Dairy Developments

The American dairy industry was one of America's first agribusinesses as we know them today, and the agricultural college and experimental farms played an important role. The Babcock butterfat test was developed and introduced by Stephen M. Babcock of the University of Wisconsin in 1890. His simple test to determine the amount of butterfat in milk accomplished more than just a standard for judging milk. It was an important contribution to the Wisconsin dairy industry at a time

The Country Gentleman, 1915.

when the dairy business was evolving from a family farm business to a milk co-op business.

Milk processing and the processing of products like butter, cheese, and casein are done most efficiently by milk co-ops, and the Babcock test enabled their formation. It allowed each farmer in the co-op to be paid an amount commensurate with the quality of the milk he contributed. And it helped dairy farmers compare the productivity of their individual cows and their overall herd. Finally, the test helped establish the credibility of scientific farming and the agricultural-extension experiment stations.

It was the dairy business that developed herd books, careful

The Country Gentleman, 1920.

records of each cow's productivity, and genetics. Since milk production was also an indication of the cow's health and breeding, records allowed today's dairy herds to be carefully selected from animals that have genetic records going back more than a century.

Dairy farmers know that keeping the girls happy means higher milk production. So it seems that the dairy farmer has always gone out of his way to provide all of the little comforts that make a cow more contented—keeping a radio on in the milking parlor, and checking to see which station the girls prefer. Dairy farmers are always testing and comparing; it's their nature. Dairy barns were the first to be air conditioned. It was a logical step and fairly economical, since the dairy barn used a large refrigeration unit for the milk coolers anyway. On the other hand agriculture researchers noticed that cows preferred loafing under shade trees rather than inside a cool barn.

Row Crops

When you meet a farmer who grows row

Fruit and vegetable harvesting were always extremely labor intensive. A fruit ladder could be nearly 20-feet long, with only one back leg for support. During the harvest season in Santa Clara Valley, everybody picked fruit—men, women, and even schoolchildren. Hired hands were always scarce and finally became so difficult to find after World War II that California farmers began to invite seasonal workers from Mexico to pick crops. *San Jose Historical Museum*

crops, you are talking with a person who spends a lot of time in his fields. "Row crops," not surprisingly, is the name used to describe those plants grown in long rows. What may not be so obvious is that row crops are often vegetables: beets, carrots, onions, garlic, radishes, lettuce, tomatoes. There are however, two significant fruits I could include: strawberries and grapes. In California's fertile Salinas Valley fields of strawberries alternate with fields of cauliflower and broccoli.

Like your own vegetable garden, row crops need constant care and supervision. The new plants are very tender and will be ruined by a late frost. Insects, weeds, or virus infections can take an entire crop. Too much rain will delay ripening or cause molds to form. A row crop farmer is in the field nearly every day, cultivating to clear the weeds, looking for pests, watering, and worrying.

Orchards

Like the rowcrop farmer, the orchardist grows a crop that is extremely labor intensive to harvest. Although the almond and walnut growers have developed machinery to pick the nuts from the trees, for the most part, pruning and picking must all be done by hand. Since this work must be done very quickly once the fruit is ripe, the orchardist has to find contract labor in a hurry. Peaches, pears, plums and apricots, sometime called the stone fruits, bruise easily. Apples and olives are a little tougher but still need to be handled with care.

Like wheat farmers, orchardists can grow only one type of crop on their land and can take regular vacations. But while the wheat farmer can get a crop the first year he plants, it takes several years before an orchardist sees any return on his investment.

Ostrich farming in San Jose, California, circa 1906. Everything old is new again. Some farmers were always trying something new and exotic; ostriches, llamas, silk worms, chinchillas. Who would have thought soybeans, sunflower seeds, safflower, or kiwi fruit would ever be so popular? *San Jose Historical Museum*

Experimental Crops

There are all sorts of new foods on American tables, fruits and vegetables that were considered exotic just a generation ago. Oranges were once a treat at Christmas; children would be more delighted to find an orange in their Christmas stocking than a giant chocolate bar. Oranges are harvested in early December and once were only available a few months of the year.

The most interesting crops, and frequently the most profitable, are the ones that are new. Pistachios, a nut that is very rich in oil, were once grown exclusively in Iran. When political unrest in Iran made it impossible to import this delicacy, orchardists in California began growing the nut for the American market.

Experimental farming is not limited to just fruits and vegetables. For example, the 1990s has seen a resurgence of interest in raising ostriches and other ratite birds for both feathers and meat. Ostrich raising was popular in Texas and California around the turn of the century to supply milliners with feathers for hats and fans, but it mostly disappeared when the market for hats and feathers dried up.

The one-time demand for fashionable kidskin gloves also produced a requirement for raising goats. Although Santa Clara Valley is usually associated with apricots, plums, and cherries, there once was a glove factory located in the heart of Silicon Valley. And in the days before animal rights and political correctness, mink and chinchilla farming were touted as lucrative businesses by the farm journals.

Hoard's Dairyman, 1926.

CHAPTER TWO

The Farmhouse

The Country Kitchen

We seem to have a romantic fascination with our farm heritage. Supermarket magazine racks are full of glossy publications with titles prominently displaying the words "country" and "country living." Somehow it must make us feel comfortable and secure to recall country life, even if we never milked a cow or fed chickens.

"Country" and other rural-sounding adjectives also find their way onto the packaged food labels in our grocery stores. There is "country-fresh" bread, "farm-fresh" eggs, "country crock" margarine, and "fresh-picked" vegetables, implying that those crisp little red radishes and that juicy corn came right out of the garden just minutes ago.

A successful farm is a cooperative business venture with all members of the family participating. So if the barn and the fields were the male domain, the house and farmyard were usually seen as the woman's area of management responsibility.

This farmer seems to be fairly prosperous judging from his two-story frame farmhouse. Farmers in Nebraska were still living in sod huts when this tidy frame house was built in neighboring Kansas. The stone mound to the left just behind the little girl is probably the storm cellar. *Halbe Collection, The Kansas State Historical Society*

It is frequently noted that women were just as capable of operating farm machinery, and many wives did heavy chores, especially during World War II, when hired help was nonexistent. But the farmhouse itself was not just an ordinary house, the place the farm family ate and slept. It, too, was an important farm building, operated and managed by the farm wife.

Country Cooking

Today's image of the farm includes the notion that traditional farm families were well-fed and they always had a selection of "farm-fresh" food on the dinner table. There seems to be a romantic fantasy that although corn or wheat or beans or tobacco was the cash crop, the average farm wife kept a vegetable garden and a small orchard that provided the raw materials for jams, pickles, and dozens of other goodies. Not to mention freshly churned butter, homemade bread, eggs gathered daily, and the fried chicken for Sunday dinner.

If there is one farm myth that continues today it is "country cooking." Suburban restaurant chains now feature down-home victuals served on gingham tablecloths with painted washboards decorating the walls. There seems to be a resurgence of apple pie and biscuits with sausage gravy on the menu, sure-fire signs that you are eating in an establishment with a "country cook" in the kitchen (or one in the advertising department).

There are some interesting contradictions in the current myths about farm cooking. One myth

Use the Maytag Multi-Motor Indoors—
No Gas — No Smoke

There are many advantages to this remarkable gas-power washer. But right now the most important is this:

In zero weather you can use the Maytag Multi-Motor Washer in the kitchen. Furthermore, you can work in perfectly clear air—because the Maytag has a long flexible metal exhaust hose which carries the exhaust gases outdoors.

Here again the wonderful Maytag Multi-Motor brings all the convenience of the finest electric washer to homes not having electricity.

Why wash by hand? Why labor and rub and work over the wash tub? This remarkable Maytag invention is operated by a wonderful little air-cooled gas engine which is a part of the plant itself. It gives you a power washer which will handle any kind of clothes. Put in your clothes, soap and hot water. Start the little motor—that's all. Then feed them through the three-way adjustable power wringer, and your wash is done.

Thousands are in use today. More are ordered every day. You find delighted users everywhere. Go see the local Maytag dealer. Have him demonstrate the machine. Costs little to buy and little to operate. See about it at once. If you do not know the local dealer, write us for his name.

THE MAYTAG COMPANY, Dept. 101, Newton, Iowa

Branches of Philadelphia, Pa.; Indianapolis, Ind.; Minneapolis, Minn.; Kansas City, Mo.; Portland, Ore.; Winnipeg, Man., Can., and The Maytag Company of England, 323 Caledonian Road, King's Cross, London

Makers of Maytag Multi-Motor, Electric, Belt and Hand Power Washers

For Homes With Electricity

For many years the Maytag Wood Tub Electric has been a tremendous favorite. It has the inherent quality for which all Maytag products are famous. It is the same in every respect as the Maytag Multi-Motor save that it is operated by a modern electric motor. Like the Multi-Motor, the Wood Tub Electric has a three-way adjustable power wringer. You merely feed the clothes through.

Maytag
Multi-Motor Washer
With Built-In Gasoline Engine

The Country Gentleman, 1921.

says that the larder was always commodious—after all, you were right there at the source of food production, and every farm had good, fresh milk, creamery butter, and newly laid eggs. Think of all the jams and jellies in the cellars, the canned fruit, and the hot bread. And, of course, there was always a smokehouse with bacon and a few hams. But other stories say that the menu was pretty monotonous in those days before reliable refrigeration. You got eggs if your chickens were laying; otherwise, breakfast was oatmeal or corn bread. Meat was old or tough or both.

Both extremes, the bountiful larder and the monotonous menu, are valid. Refrigeration was a luxury before World War II. Even in town, most houses still had iceboxes—heavily insulated chests with drip pans underneath—until after 1946. On a warm day the ice melted and the inattentive housewife would find her kitchen floor flooded by an overflowing drip pan. The farm wife did a lot of canning, but so did the ladies in town. Fruits and vegetables were put up in jars and stored in the pantry or cellar. Even meats were canned and preserved in jars and a fermenting crock of "minced meat" sat in our cellar all year-round.

I remember that farm kitchens all seemed to be three times as large as the kitchens of the houses in town. The "country kitchen" layouts that the interior designers like to show in magazines today neglect

Canning vegetables in a homestead kitchen in rural Austin, Minnesota, 1936. *Paul Carter photo, Library of Congress, FSA*

FIG. 127. A kitchen pump, sink and drain pipe in the kitchens should cost not more than $15, and get result in immeasurable saving of time, energy and health.

A hand pump at the kitchen sink was an incredible convenience in the days before true "indoor plumbing."

to show all the reasons for the extra space. I remember that the farm kitchen was frequently a nursery for small animals that were ailing or just puny. Chicken eggs were brought in to incubate under the stove, and sometimes a box of kittens or even a calf was brought inside where it was warmer.

Most kitchen tables and most dining room tables, too, had an oilcloth cover for everyday use. Tablecloths and napkins were reserved for holidays. The farm wife had enough laundry to do without ironing linen. And I have never encountered anyone, in story or in person, who lived on a farm and had someone come in to wash the laundry.

Country Gentleman Recipes

There was a wonderful article on food and cooking titled "Some of Grandmother's Good Things" in the September 1916 issue of *The Country Gentleman*. It takes the form of a letter from a woman to her niece.

Dear Janet:

I am ashamed that you have had to write the fourth time for some of the good things your grandmother was famous for. You really ought to be more interested in "general principles than in specific recipes" as is so often asserted in the classroom, but we women are all alike, I suspect. We capture a good recipe when we get a chance and do not bother our heads very much about principles.

Your grandma was a born cook, and that beats a made cook every time. She was famous for her warmed-up potatoes—they were far better than when first cooked. To a quart of cold cooked potatoes she took a tablespoonful of fat, preferably bacon fat, and seasoning well with salt and pepper, she allowed them to heat slowly as she chopped them with a tin can with holes in the bottom. When thoroughly heated—most people do not allow time enough in warming up—she added half a cupful of sour cream—sweet will do, but the flavor of sour is better. She always tasted her potatoes, the seasoning and the heating being the essential factors. It takes more time than you think to heat up potatoes properly.

At home as a boy, Ben always had graham bread on the table. You had better write his mother for her recipe. There are a good many different ones, but the one your grandmother worked out herself I like better than any other I have tried. When grandmother was a young woman the "graham movement" swept the country. Grahamites were as thick as blackberries in some localities. Absurd claims were made for graham bread, and as it was not a cure for all the ills human flesh is heir to, a reaction unfortunately set in. Graham bread is good, very good; due to its laxative qualities it is almost indispensable for some people, so I would plan to have it on the table most of the time, but I would use a variety of recipes and in that way get more of it eaten. Most people tire of it unless it is served in different ways.

GRANDMOTHER'S GRAHAM BREAD: Half a cake of dry yeast, soaked in half a cupful of tepid water; into three cupfuls of hot water beat four cupfuls of white flour, one tablespoon of sugar, one tablespoon of salt, two tablespoons of lard. Add the yeast, let rise overnight, then add four cupfuls of graham flour, half a cupful of sugar, one cupful of shaved nut meats. Put at once into two tins four inches by eight inches on the bottom and not less than three inches deep. Let rise till the pans are full, then bake slowly.

Your grandmother used to make a cheese pudding, of which your father is extremely fond: Two cupfuls of dried bread—diced—two and a half cupfuls of milk, yolks of four eggs, two teaspoonfuls of salt, two teaspoonfuls of baking powder. Beat all thoroughly together, add the stiffly beaten egg whites of four eggs, pour into a buttered baking dish, set into a pan of hot water, bake twenty to thirty minutes or till stiffened all through. Serve at once. I will take up entertaining on the farm in my next letter. Your affectionate,

Aunt Nellie

Feeding the chickens was usually the first chore that small children were assigned. This pair has stayed on to play with the chicks. *Halbe Collection, The Kansas State Historical Society*

On our farm with just two cows, separating milk was done in the kitchen and on the adjacent screened porch. Sanitation was critical when handling milk, and the cans could not be washed with soap; they were sanitized daily with scalding hot water. Heating the water, moving the buckets around, and scalding the milk cans took a little space.

Canning and sausage-making took a fair amount of space, too, and frequently a separate canning kitchen was set up. This was due in great part to the fact that canning was hot work, done in late summer when fruits and

vegetables were at their peak of ripeness. And canning meant that big pans of boiling water were sanitizing the glass jars and the lids, while other big cookers used for "processing" were steaming away. If men had threshing circles to help with harvesting, women frequently had canning clubs or sewing circles to help out when necessary.

Our kitchen had some fairly heavy scales on which to weigh baskets of produce or chickens. Though the meat butchering was done elsewhere, chickens were a completely different story.

The Farmer's Wife, 1912.

Egg Money

The rooster crows but the hen delivers.

The farm magazines all have stories about how a well-managed flock of chickens has managed to make enough money to pay for a college education or a trip to Europe. The articles encourage farm women to think of poultry raising as a business rather than a hobby. While the Roaring Twenties are usually seen as a time of economic growth in America, times were hard for the farmers. Raising chickens was a quick way to get some additional cash.

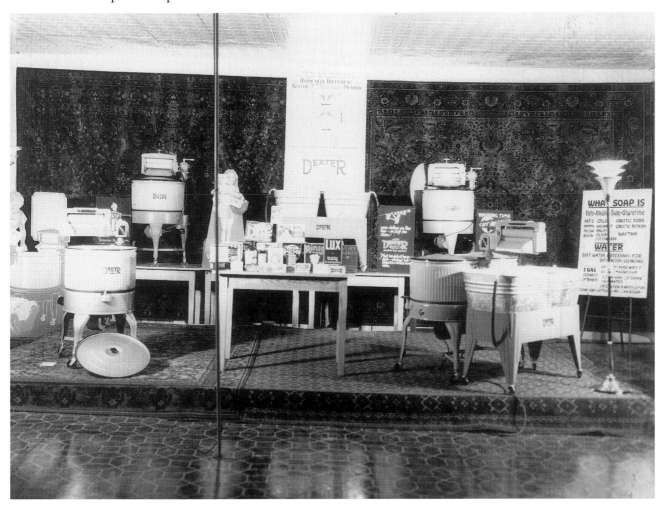

Washing machine demonstration, designed to make you want to sign up for a new Dexter washer. But most housewives considered the washing machine to be extravagant and still cleaned clothes by boiling or scrubbing on a washboard. Early machines were designed to swish clothes around a tub and did nothing to relieve the drudgery of hauling hot water and then moving the heavy, wet garments from the wash tub to rinse tubs and then to the clotheslines. When indoor plumbing finally included a hot water heater, the sales of washing machines skyrocketed. *Ritzville Public Library*

An imposing farmhouse with a pleasant tree shading the porch in the back, circa 1900. But even this large, comfortable looking home has the sanitary facilities in a separate building; the "little house" is just to the left of the big house. *Ritzville Public Library*

Measuring Up

The April 1924 issue of *Farm Journal* had a little survey of farm homes in the Orange township of Blackhawk County, Iowa, just south of the town of Waterloo. The survey was prompted by a civic-improvement campaign and the article challenges readers to see how well their community measures up against Orange. It's interesting to note that while every farm holder took the newspaper, only 24 percent had indoor toilets and fewer than half had running water piped in. The article does not mention how many farmers had radios and how many had power tractors.

There were

- 142 homes in the township
- 142 with newspaper or magazine subscriptions
- 132 with telephones
- 80 with pianos
- 79 with automobiles
- 63 with gas or electric lights
- 47 with bathrooms
- 34 with indoor toilets

And it wasn't just limited to the 1920s and 1930s. An article by W. R. Whitfield of the Iowa State College Extension office in the October 1952 *Farm Journal* says that an acre of chickens made as much money as 20 acres of his other crops. Whitfield reports that farmer L. J. Kuhn had a problem; he had only 160 acres and wanted to increase his income. Instead of getting more land, he decided to turn to a crop with a higher yield. His solution was to raise chickens.

He turned two acres of his 160-acre farm over to poultry. That's the space it took for the chicken house and range. Two acres of chickens produced as much money as any other 40 acres on the place. Chickens added a fifth to the size of his farm's income, grossing $3,497.

The farmer was always encouraged to think about the business of farming, the cost of production balanced against the profit in the marketplace, and so was his wife. The women's pages in nearly every farm magazine discuss the same cost-benefit relationship in poultry production. Poultry raising was always seen as women's work, and poultry raisers were encouraged to keep track of expenses, get rid of poor producers, and raise the quality of the product.

Guess the Price
of this Handsome
Sterling Home!

Here is the *exact picture* of a model *Sterling Home*—the "Senator." It is just as fine as it looks. Eight large rooms and four large closets. Guess the cash price! Guess what the complete building materials cost — *including lumber, plaster, hardware, paint, nails, etc.*

Three thousand dollars? No, *less than that!* Two thousand dollars? No, less than that! Fifteen hundred? No, *less than that!* One thousand dollars? Less than that! *Write for the Sterling Book and see*

there—the amazing price with complete floor plan and specifications. And this is but *one* of the famous fifty Sterling Models, ranging from $250 to $2500. The other forty-nine are equally *low priced.*

STERLING
System Built
HOMES

Remember, too, that these prices include all the ready-cut features. Every *timber* and *board* has been *measured* and *cut-to-fit* in our mammoth factory, which has *6000 capacity per season.* That saves *you over half the labor cost,* which is usually a greater expense than the total cost of lumber.

Furthermore, we give *liberal credit* to Home Builders—*something that no similar concern has ever offered.* You can make a reasonable cash payment and pay balance in small, monthly installments covering a period of *two years.*

All Sterling Lumber is cut from the *rim of the log*—no soft or rotten spots, no warped lumber—no unsightly knots—no blemishes of *any* kind. We own vast forests as well as immense mills, so can *guarantee* first quality lumber. We have mills and shipping stations in Michigan, Florida, Texas and Washington. No trouble to deliver quickly, regardless of your location. Complete *Plans, Blue Prints* and *Chart of Instructions* accompany each job. So simple that anyone can build now without hiring expert mechanics.

THE "MIRACLE"—One of the most remarkable ever designed—Living Room and Dining Room—two large bedrooms—bath—model, work-saving kitchen. Fine Porch, all complete. Can be erected in 12 to 14 days. $414 down, balance, $11.51 per month. Total cost, $801.

Farm Building Bargains

Our barn and building proposition, if possible, is even better than our Home Offer. Modern and practical to the last detail and strong as Gibraltar. Easy to erect, for all lumber comes ready-cut. And we include *Blue Prints, Plans,* etc. Most farmers do the erecting themselves, without the cost of carpenter work.

Any *type* of farm building you want, any *size,* any *price.* Eighty barns, ten hog houses, fifteen poultry houses, implement sheds, corn cribs, etc. And what prices! Far lower than usual. From $75 to $1500.

To get our latest Barn and Building Book, mark a cross in the square, on coupon, opposite "Farm Building Book."

An Extraordinary Book

Our latest book, the "Famous Fifty," has become a nation-wide sensation. We receive as high as 3000 requests for it in a *single* day's mail.

Don't miss it! Don't buy or contract to buy a home at any price or on *any terms* till you have seen the most astounding Home Book we have ever published.

Use the Coupon below, or a letter or postal.

INTERNATIONAL MILL AND TIMBER CO.
Dept. A 5
BAY CITY, MICH.

STERLING
SYSTEM BUILT

HOM

BOOK COUPON

International Mill & Timber Company
Dept. A 5, Bay City, Mich.
Gentlemen: I expect to build soon. Please send me your

☐ HOME BUILDER'S BOOK.
☐ BOOK ON FARM BUILDINGS.

Name...

My address is...

Be sure to mark which book you want. If you want both, mark both squares.

The Country Gentleman, 1915.

The larder was frequently an adjacent root cellar, used for storing jars of fruit and vegetables that had been canned during the summer. Cellars like this, dug into the ground and covered with earth were also used to shelter families from tornadoes or dangerous windstorms. Itasca County, Minnesota. *John Vachon photo, Library of Congress, FSA*

Along with indoor plumbing, probably the other single biggest difference between farm folks and city folks was keeping chickens. The gentry just couldn't be bothered to chase after chickens. It was a lot easier, cleaner, and cheaper to buy a dozen eggs and a cut-up fryer at the supermarket. In the good old days—and these are the days of less than a generation ago—chickens were a seasonal food, like fruit and vegetables.

Chickens tend to lay the most eggs in the spring and early summer, fewer eggs in the fall. They go into an annual molt in the fall, losing their feathers and growing new ones to keep them warm in the winter. So the chicken flock was culled in the fall and the poor producers were killed, cleaned, and canned in glass jars.

These days chickens are bred only for eggs, for frying, for roasting, or for McDonald's restaurants. It is now the age of specialization. But in the old days, just last week, every chicken was expected to lay eggs, and those that could no longer produce an egg a day went into the stew pot. Young males were never given a chance; their only career choices were fryer or roaster, depending on how much weight they gained.

One of the first chores for any farm child was to feed and water the chickens and gather the eggs.

How to Pluck a Bird

Agnes Bird, now living in Grant's Pass, Oregon, is retired from farming but maintains an active interest in rural life. She wrote this essay for her "city friends" who had never cleaned a chicken. She confessed that although she was raised in rural Oklahoma, she was a city child and did not become a farmer until she married one. Even then, Agnes says was so inexpert at catching, killing, and cleaning chickens that her mother-in-law prohibited her participation.

There were different methods of killing a chicken: either head-chopping or neck-wringing. My mother stepped on the neck with all her weight, held the bird in her hands, gave a quick jerk, then released it to flop on the ground until it was still.

My mother-in-law's college degree was in domestic science, so her methods were more scientific. There was a large cottonwood stump in the back yard with two large nails driven partway into the top, about 1-1/2 inches apart. The chicken's neck was placed between the nails, the body pulled back so the neck stretched, and then the head was chopped off with a hatchet. The bird was immediately placed headfirst (headless first?) into a "shot-gun" pail, a tall, slender, galvanized pail originally used for separating cream. This was to prevent the bird from moving and bruising his flesh.

When the bird was still, it was put in a clean bucket and covered with nearly boiling water. After being doused up and down in the water several times, the chicken was lifted out and the feathers quickly removed with the hands. An experienced chicken plucker could denude a bird in only two or three swipes. Some more stubborn chickens had pinfeathers, which had to be removed with a tweezers or the tip of a knife.

Finally, the chicken had to be singed over a flame to remove the fine hairs. After singeing, the chicken was finally ready to be drawn and dressed for cooking, another process that is now as unknown as butchering. My mother-in-law was adamant about never soaking a plucked or dressed chicken in water. It should be handled quickly and carefully to keep it as clean as possible during dressing, then wiped with a damp cloth if necessary. All the nutrients and flavors are water soluble and will be lost if the chicken is soaked or washed.

Chickens were usually the first farm animals that children were assigned to manage. If you did well, you "graduated" to a calf. "Up with the chickens" really means "up with the rooster" because it's the noisy rooster that is the farmer's alarm clock. And it's one of the chores that usually has to be done before breakfast if you want a cackling fresh egg.

Custer County, Nebraska, in 1887 was flat and treeless. The house is a "soddy," with walls built of sod bricks and a sod roof. Sod was a common building material where timber was nonexistent. It was cheap and plentiful but these benefits were balanced by a few serious drawbacks. Sod was heavy, absorbed moisture, and was home sweet home to crickets, ants, spiders, and other prairie critters. A thunderstorm could produce enough rain to cause a sod roof or wall to collapse, usually immediately after all the aforementioned creatures had abandoned their flooded home for the homesteader's hearth. Despite its otherwise crude appearance, this farm has a fine windmill and water pump. The storm cellar, can be seen directly behind the windmill. *Solomon D. Butcher Collection, Nebraska State Historical Society*

We had a hen house near the farmyard and the hens were usually fed outdoors in their pen. The technique was to enter the pen, making sure the fence was latched behind you. Put your bucket of mash in the feeder and make sure the water trough was full. Then unfasten the latch from the hen house door, open the door wide and stand aside. A flurry of chickens would come rushing out the door, heading for the mash. Then you could sneak inside the hen house and check the nesting boxes to see if the layers had produced something. Sometimes a setting hen was still on her little throne and would resent a cold hand underneath her bustle, searching for a fresh, warm egg.

Chickens could sometimes be a little difficult to manage, but they were less trouble than piglets or lambs, and they were the farm animal that provided a cushion against really hard times. Not only were the eggs and chickens important to the farm diet, it was frequently mama's "egg money" that provided a financial cushion in hard times.

Whose Chores, Anyway?

How were the chores divided? They seemed to be pretty traditional; the men did the outside work and the women did the housework. But many women also seemed to take on the heavier chores of farming, especially during World War II. The debate about who does what has gone on for years. An article in *The Country Gentleman* from September 1916 is interesting because it not only gives us a good idea of what the standard chores are, but the division of labor seems to follow the Mason-Dixon line rather than the gender line.

Should the farmer milk, feed the calves, tend the pigs and care for the hens and raise the chicks, or make his wife do it? Customs vary widely with different parts of the country. Even hoeing out the weedy garden is debatable work. A woman subscriber writes: "I am much blocked up in my housework. It seems as though I can never get done. I have four children the oldest 11, the youngest two-and-a-half-years old. I have also 100 old hens, 100 chicks, two pigs, a cow and a calf, and have to feed, milk, churn, wash, can, cook and bake, beside the regular housework!"

Heaven help! She is a brave woman. Take the one item of the washing and ironing for the man and woman and four young children in hot weather. A woman of significant means would want helpers to get through the program of our correspondent as follows: A cook, a second girl, a laundress two or three days a week, and a nurse girl, and then she would have to take the rest cure at a private sanitarium once in a while. Three cheers for our brave and plucky woman! But is it a square deal to make her raise all that livestock while she is rearing four children? Would it not be a fairer division for the man to care for the animals outside if she cares for the youngsters inside?

In the North the rule generally is for the man to do all the milking, care for the cattle, and feed the calves and the pigs, and often do the heavy work of the poultry. In the South the men as a rule do not do the milking or other small chores apart from the care of the horses and mules. Of course there are exceptions, both North and South, but generally speaking, what is "woman's work" in one section is "man's work" in the other. Now the only just thing is to ignore custom in this matter and let the husband and wife make a study of

Neighborizing the Farmer

One of the most significant facts of our telephone progress is that one-fourth of the 9,000,000 telephones in the Bell System are rural.

In the days when the telephone was merely a "city convenience," the farms of the country were so many separated units, far removed from the centers of population, and isolated by distance and lack of facilities for communication.

But, as the telephone reached out beyond cities and towns, it completely transformed farm life. It created new rural neighborhoods here, there and everywhere.

Stretching to the farthest corners of the states, it brought the remotest villages and isolated places into direct contact with the larger communities.

Today, the American farmer enjoys the same facilities for instant, direct communication as the city dweller. Though distances between farms are reckoned in miles as the crow flies, the telephone brings every one as close as next door. Though it be half a day's journey to the village, the farmer is but a telephone call away.

Aside from its neighborhood value, the telephone keeps the farmer in touch with the city and abreast of the times.

The Bell System has always recognized rural telephone development as an essential factor of Universal Service. It has co-operated with the farmer to achieve this aim.

The result is that the Bell System reaches more places than there are post offices and includes as many rural telephones as there are telephones of all kinds in Great Britain, France and Germany combined.

 AMERICAN TELEPHONE AND TELEGRAPH COMPANY
AND ASSOCIATED COMPANIES

One Policy   One System   Universal Service

The Country Gentleman, 1915.

Radio, the New Hired Man

Power Farming, 1922.

how much work it takes to run the establishment indoors and out, and then measure as sympathetically as possible their combined working power and "divvy on the square." Really, the surest index to a man's advancement in civilization is his eagerness to shift the burdens off his wife's slenderer shoulders onto his own broader ones.

Custom decrees that some very, very light work is "man's work" and some very, very heavy work—for instance, lugging the water for the washing—is "women's work." Really, it is time for a new deal. A most pertinent question right now on most farms is, "Whose chores, anyway?"

The Farm Wife Gets a Hired Hand—Maytag

It was a surprise to discover, when I first started doing research on farm tractors, that nearly all of the

largest tractor manufacturers also built washing machines at one time or another. I know there was a practical reason for this: some major tractor builders sold small stationary engines that were used to power feed mills or water pumps. And the little kerosene engines could also be used to power a washing machine. But it was obviously a good strategy in the sales and marketing department. When the farmer went to town and spent $1,000 on a new tractor, it was a good idea to spend another $50 to buy a first-class washing machine for the little woman.

Washing was a major chore and was usually done one day a week unless there was a baby or small child in the household. Then the housewife washed diapers and baby clothes on several days. Washing meant boiling buckets and buckets of water to fill the wash tubs. Really filthy clothes were sanitized by boiling. Before indoor plumbing and hot water heaters, all the wash water had to be heated on the kitchen stove.

Scrubbing clothes meant working up a suds with homemade lye soap and rubbing the soiled article on a corrugated washboard. Although both of my grandmothers used prepared laundry soap from the grocery store, they also kept a supply of homemade lye soap for the really dirty items. Lye soap and boiling water both burned the skin, and many farm wives had scars from household burns. But the toughest part of laundry was not necessarily the scrubbing; it was lugging the heavy buckets of boiling water to the wash tub and then carrying baskets of wet laundry to the clothesline.

Technology helped the farm wife, too, although the changes might not seem as obvious as

This substantial farm near Hays, Kansas, was built before 1900. The entire family has lined up for the photographer who has had to set up his camera a quarter mile down the road to be able to include all the important features. Mom and Pop are standing beside the front porch. There are five children in the driveway. And there appear to be two ranch hands standing in front of the barns. *Halbe Collection, The Kansas State Historical Society*

having a new tractor roll up to the door. When mechanization made plowing easier, it also made laundry day a little easier. If the housewife could not afford a washing machine she at least had a roller wringer. Actually, sometimes the presence of a washing machine was not related to expense, it was related to prejudice. The woman in charge felt that a washing machine did not get her clothing clean enough. So the washboard, the boiling pot, and

Watch the Crop Reports with a Day-Fan Radio

The Country Gentleman, 1926.

High water or high wind, both were treacherous. This farm house, barn, and shed were carried away by a flooding creek. Farmers could be caught, unaware of the potential flood danger when spring runoff or a storm miles away suddenly turned a quiet creek into a killing torrent. Disaster relief for farmers was unknown until recent times. *The Kansas State Historical Society*

good, strong lye soap were better than any machine.

The procedure of washing the white clothes first, then the colored articles, and scrubbing the really grimy work clothes last was necessary in that time when the same wash water was reused for the entire laundry—only the rinse water was changed.

Putting Food By—Pickles, Preserves, and Produce

Farm magazines and journals had always included a few articles specifically addressing food preservation. An 1865 issue of the *American Agriculturalist* has a department enti-

This ornate detail decorates a prosperous Ohio Valley farm. Well-to-do farmers could afford large, comfortable homes with ornate construction details, stained glass windows, and an organ in the parlor. We should remember that many folks with a business in town also lived on a farm, especially if they operated a farm-related business such as an implement dealership or a seed store. A showplace farm with a beautiful house and impressive barn was just good advertising.

tled "The Household," with long articles on vinegar making, coloring cheese, and the preparation of cool drinks for summer. The want ads also offered products for the farm wife, ranging from the practical to the fanciful. There are ads in these early farm journals for new sewing machines and butter churns and ads for hair crimpers and piano music. Mrs. Henry Ward Beecher is listed in a testimonial, recommending a new clothes wringer. It would be several more decades before any inexpensive and functional washing machines appeared.

Nutrition as a science was first established just after the Civil War by Wilbur O. Atwater, acting as the first director of the Office of the Experiment Stations for the U. S. Department of Agriculture. Atwater was trained as a chemist, and his special interest was to compare various types of food—corn kernels, for example—and determine which variety of corn kernel contained the most water, the most protein, and the most sugar. He also compared the places where a specific crop was grown, demonstrating that different soils can affect the composition of the crops.

The Sunbonnet Babies have hot school-lunches.
By Bertha Corbett Melcher

On cold winter days when the snow
Seems to make our appetites grow,
We serve soup to all, good and hot,
Which each one says "just hits the spot!"

With a big chicken sandwich or two,
Um! good every mouthful you chew!
And a big rosy apple to munch,
Naught can surpass the noon lunch.

The Sunbonnet Babies were a regular feature in *The Farmer's Wife* and were such a favorite that they decorated not only magazines and books but also china patterns, needlework designs, and quilt patterns. *The Farmer's Wife, 1912*

Kiddies Kanning Klubs

Food preservation and food preparation were established in the agricultural colleges as part of the curriculum, and many of the university field offices were extremely active in promoting and demonstrating new techniques. Food and nutrition demonstrators met with farm women, showing them easier ways to preserve and use the fruits and vegetables they had canned. So when farmers were developing efficient food-production methods, their wives were also maturing a new scientific industry: nutrition and home economics. Farm children were also involved in projects to train them for careers in food production or processing. While many children kept a garden or raised 4-H animals to show at the fair, some had other interests, such as canning clubs.

In addition to the women's pages, the farm magazines had a few pages devoted to games, puzzles, and projects for farm youth. *The Country Gentleman* of September 1916 details a few "reliable" recipes developed by the Federal States Relation Service, Office of Extension Work, just for the use of boys' and girls' home-canning clubs. (Remember that killing, cleaning, and cooling a chicken is already a half-day's work.) An example follows.

POULTRY AND GAME: Kill fowl and draw at once; wash carefully and cool: cut into convenient sections. Place in wire basket or cheesecloth and boil until meat can be removed from the bones; lift it from the boiling liquid, and remove meat from bones; pack closely into glass jars; fill the jars with pot liquid after it has been concentrated to half its volume; add a level teaspoonful of salt to a quart of meat for seasoning; put rubber and cap in position, not tight; and sterilize the length of time given below for the one particular type of outfit you are using:

- Water bath, homemade or
  commercial: 3-1/2 hours
- Water seal, 214 degrees: 3 hours
- 5 pounds steam pressure: 2-1/2 hours
- 10 to 15 pounds steam pressure:
  1-1/2 hours

Remove jars; tighten covers; invert to cool and test the joint; and wrap jars with paper to prevent bleaching.

Rural Communication
The Radio

Farmers got a tractor and a radio about the same time and suddenly the world became a market. The radio brought two wonderful and important pieces of information to the farmer every day: the weather and the current market prices. Weather forecasting was unheard of; the farmer might just as well step outside and look up in the sky. Or consult a passing groundhog. But the weatherman could report about yesterday's weather with 100 percent accuracy, anyplace in the United States. And information about freezing conditions for Florida citrus or rain on Kansas wheat might affect the price his crop would bring in Chicago next week.

Radio first arrived about the end of World War I, but receivers were not widely available until the early 1920s. Once they appeared, however, they were widely accepted and suitable programming quickly became available. Radio manufacturer Atwater Kent announced the completion of his millionth radio set in 1926. Kent also sponsored the Atwater Kent music hour, which allowed farmers and anyone else with a radio receiver to now listen to at least one hour of performances of the finest opera and concert stars.

Buying a radio receiver was a powerful incentive to install electricity. Farmers quickly saw the benefit of hearing the weather and the commodity prices in the major markets. But the radio brought entertainment, too. I don't remember many farmers, especially the older ones, spending their evenings with a farm magazine or a book. And rural television was not around until after 1960 or so and then only with a superior antenna. But farmers sat around on the porch and listened to the radio after supper when the chores were done.

Two Longs and One Short—the Party Line

On my grandparents' rural route, nearly all the phone "subscribers" on their road and a few others were on the same telephone line. Everyone on that line was assigned a code on the ringer bell. You cranked the bell handle on the side of the phone to call a neighbor. If I wanted to call Mrs. Wilkins I just cranked her code, one long ring and two short ones.

When I cranked a long and two shorts, all the telephones up and down the road would also ring and everybody on the road would know that the Wilkinses were getting a call. So even though I wanted to ask Mrs. Wilkins a question, another neighbor might come on the line and say, "Mrs. Wilkins went to town this morning. I saw her drive past about an hour ago." There was no privacy, and while it was considered very rude to interrupt or to eavesdrop, people still did it.

If you had to make a call to someone in town, you had to call the switchboard operator, and she would connect you to the cable that went to town. Many of the operators had the telephone switchboards in their homes and were awakened in the middle of the night if there was an emergency. The Bell Telephone System was mostly a telephone network for the big cities. Phone service in the little towns was frequently overlooked because the customers were so few and so far between.

A pretty average winter in the Midwest. In the really big storms the snow would be up to the windows on the second floor. Farmers would dig a snow tunnel out to the barn to feed the livestock. *Halbe Collection, The Kansas State Historical Society*

CHAPTER THREE

The Barnyard

The Kitchen Garden

It was mother's pride and children's punishment, the kitchen garden. It was usually hot and boring work. We were each outfitted in an exceptionally ugly sun hat of some sort and sent out to weed and hoe the vegetable garden. Helping in the garden meant finding the fat tomato worms, pulling the beetles off the beans and looking for corn borers. Freeloading pests were dropped in a coffee can with a little kerosene in the bottom. We preferred to find a few of these pests and then take them over to the chicken yard, providing tasty treats for the chickens.

Miss Nan Bartz had a lot of chickens, a few ducks, and several turkeys. She also has a small companion who has taken refuge on the hen house roof. Many farmers raised a variety of fowl to suit every need and occasion; a three-pound fryer for dinner or a six-pound roaster if the parson was coming to Sunday dinner. And why not raise a few turkeys for Thanksgiving if you had enough room in the poultry pen? For every fancier who had a preference for only Rhode Island Reds or Buff Orpingtons, there were farmers who liked a selection. My grandfather raised ducks for a number of years, simply because it amused him to watch them waddle down to the pond.
Solomon D. Butcher Collection, Nebraska State Historical Society

A farmstead in central Kansas, with cattle grazing out in the fields to the left. A family of five people stands in front of the porch. The fence posts are especially interesting. Many treeless areas of Kansas use dressed limestone as posts, a unique solution where limestone is plentiful and trees are scarce. *Halbe Collection, The Kansas State Historical Society*

We were luckier than most of our compatriots because we were not trusted to weed the garden until the plants were already bearing. We couldn't tell the difference between sweet peas and bindweeds. And by the time the plants were mature enough for us to easily see the difference, they were so large there was almost no benefit in weeding. But we were always detailed to go pick pea pods, green beans, squash, corn, or tomatoes.

There were always a number of suitable kitchen chores for small children. Feeding the chickens and gathering eggs were usually a child's first barnyard responsibilities. There were always beans to snap or peas to shell. The butter churn was operated by kid power; usually a small boy could be tricked into churning by an adult's mentioning that turning the churn promoted masculine muscle building.

The Difference between Chores and Work

My 10-year-old son and my dad were discussing Saturday's schedule. "You mean I have to do all that work before I can play?" whined my son.

"Work? That's not work," replied my dad.

"It's not? It sure sounds like work."

"Nope," Dad replied. "That's not work, son, it's chores. I wouldn't make you work on a

This is a real milkmaid with her cow and her little pail. The photographer has written "Nebraska lassie" under the brindle cow, but he is undoubtedly referring to the little girl. She is identified as Alice T. Butcher, on the farm near Middle Loup, West Union, Nebraska. *Solomon D. Butcher Collection, Nebraska State Historical Society*

Saturday. But chores—those are the things you just have to do every day."

So there you have it. Farm chores were the routine responsibilities that had to be done every day, rain or shine, summer or winter. First thing in the morning, feed the livestock, check their water, and turn them out to pasture. Milk the cows. Then you can think about coming in and eating breakfast yourself. I always think of chores as those tasks that were done around the barnyard.

Yard Dogs and Barn Cats

Pets were discouraged, I suppose, because so many of the farm animals were destined for market. Cats and dogs were common barnyard company, but they did not come in the house; they each had their place and their responsibility in the farmyard. Small animals were sometimes nursed in the farm kitchen, or an ailing child might have a kitten allowed in for amusement, but by and large, no pets were allowed in the house.

There were only two kinds of dogs on the farm, hunting dogs and yard dogs. Too valuable to run loose, hunting dogs were kept penned or chained unless they were extraordinarily trustworthy. Otherwise, they might head to the poultry yard for a little amusement. The yard dog was usually some sort of mutt, kept to announce strangers and intimidate salesmen. The yard dog had to have good sense and good manners, stay out of the way of the equipment and livestock, and never, never, never chase chickens.

Dogs running loose were shot, and there was no discussion about this. Not only was a loose pack of dogs a hazard to lambs and calves, but dogs were apt to encounter diseased raccoons or woodchucks. Because stray dogs could bring all sorts of trouble to a farm, farmers were especially wary of canines that might wander in looking for a handout. Dogs with good manners might get taken on as yard dogs, others just seemed to disappear. A stray dog looking for a situation would hang around a few days while the family looked him over. If he fit in, there might be a position for him.

Cats and kittens also had specific chores. Their job was to keep mice and rats out of the corn crib. The cat population around our farm seemed to be somewhat constant and the cats were very independent, preferring to hunt in the fields beyond the pasture. Cats came and went, but that is their nature. The cats on our farm also ate insects, catching and crunching grasshoppers on the fly. Some farmers had a strong aversion to cats and instead would encourage barn owls to nest to keep rodents under control in the barn.

The little house behind the little house behind the big house. The lady of the house wears a "poke" bonnet and heavy gloves while feeding her chickens. A poke bonnet was more useful than a straw hat which could blow around unless it was securely tied. And another benefit of the poke or "bag"—that loose fabric behind the brim—was that you could use it as a place to carry eggs or berries or other important items that one might encounter while rambling around the farm. I recall that once my bonnet was especially useful to trap tadpoles, but of course, it was unwearable the rest of the afternoon. *Ritzville Public Library Collection*

Water, Wells, and Windmills

How long will a windmill last? An article from the *Farm Journal* of September 1937 says that, with proper maintenance, a windmill can last for years. It reports that F. M. Atteberry, who lives near Pathfinder Irrigation District in Nebraska, has a mill and tower, in use since 1910, that pumps water for between 500 and 800 head of stock. The mill has always been kept in repair and the windmill and pump have been in service for 27 years.

Farm house and water tower on the Grant Ranch, Mount Hamilton, California. Now part of the Santa Clara County regional park system, the Grant Ranch was once a prosperous cattle raising operation in the foothills of Silicon Valley. Tank towers are typical landmarks in California where the windmills once pumped water to large redwood tanks on platforms 20 or 30 feet above the ground. Since the temperate climate kept the water from freezing, raising the tank allowed sufficient water pressure to serve indoor plumbing without constant pumping.

Windmills meant water; water meant a productive farm. Daniel Hallady is credited with introducing the windmill to America in 1854, and these early wooden windmills can only be seen in museums today. The windmill was redesigned and built of steel and sheet metal by Stuart Perry in 1883. Steel windmills were cheap and reliable and therefore quickly became widespread. There were dozens of windmill companies, many of them in Indiana, Illinois, and the Ohio Valley, all of them building steel windmills at the turn of the century.

Wind-powered pumps were gradually replaced by small portable gas engines or generators. When the rural-electrification programs were carried out during the 1930s and 1940s by the federal government, even more windmills were replaced by small electric pumps. But a windmill is still the preferred method of providing water to livestock in distant pastures, where it may be too expensive or too impractical to run an electrical line to power a pump.

The windmill design consists of a number of small vanes set radially in a wheel. Governing is automatic: of yaw by the tail vane, and of torque by setting the wheel off-center with respect to the vertical yaw axis. Thus, as the wind increases, the mill turns on its vertical axis, reducing the effective area and therefore its speed.

A windmill in the barnyard is an important indicator of the presence of water. Looking at the old pictures of early farmsteads, the windmill not only tells us the direction of the wind, it says that this farmer could use wind power to pump water. Since good water is the most important and essential single element to farm prosperity, the presence of a windmill and tower in the barnyard usually says that water is accessible. Adequate clean water had to be available to keep livestock. There were parts of western Kansas where it was easier to bathe in whiskey than water.

Vast stretches of Texas, Oklahoma, Kansas, and Colorado were uninhabitable until very recently because water was scarce. And what little water could be found was so awful that cattle wouldn't drink it.

Smokehouse, Springhouse, and Corn Crib

There were several other barnyard buildings that deserve mention because they are so common,

although not all of them were in widespread use. The smokehouse was used to cure meats, especially game if someone in the family actually went hunting. Smoking meat was not a widespread practice on most farms during my youth although there were still a lot of smokehouses around. Ours was the same shape and size as a privy, and every now and then a guest would head for the smokehouse and have to be

redirected to the indoor facilities. We used our smokehouse for storing some of the garden tools. We took our meat down to the locker in town, and if someone had meat to smoke, that went down to the meat locker, too. It was cheaper and easier.

The springhouse was a small rock or concrete shed built over a running spring. It was used as a cooler or refrigerator before iceboxes were generally

Yard dog or hunting hound—this animal looks like a combination of both. Dogs had to know their place on a farm. *Ritzville Public Library*

available. Since it was popular as a watering hole for small animals, the spring house had to be approached with some caution.

The other universal building on the farm was the corn crib, a structure that came in a variety of sizes and shapes. It was used to dry and store corn on the cob that was used for animal feed. Some cribs looked like miniature silos, round tanks made out of corrugated sheet metal. Others were built out of wood lathe with enough space between the slats to allow the corn to dry. Somewhere close to the corn crib was a corn sheller, a hand-cranked grinding device that removed the kernels from the cobs. But if we were going to give the chickens a quick treat, we just shelled the corn by hand, rubbing two ears of dried corn together until the kernels popped off.

Storm Cellars

If you went to the outhouse armed with a fly swatter, storm cellars required a broom for one's protection. Built as an occasional safety shelter for use during tornadoes, the storm cellar frequently served a function between storms as a sort of subterranean pantry. Havens for

vermin, most storm cellars were used to store canned goods, along with potatoes, apples, and other produce.

Many farmhouses were built with cellars underneath the house, but sometimes a high water table precluded digging a pit under the house. A storm cellar was always a good idea on the high plains to provide shelter during a cyclone or high wind. Sometimes it was just a shallow cellar with soil mounded up over the roof to deflect the wind. Since the cellar was the coolest place on the farm, it was frequently whitewashed inside, lined with shelves, and used for

The CountryGentleman, 1920.

TENANCY

THE FARM HAND

THE LURE OF THE CITY

THE CHANCE TO COME INTO THE LAND-OWNING CLASS

BIG WAGES AND THE GAY LIFE

The tidy farmyard of Ivan and June Lotenvitz near Charles, City Iowa. Ivan was born on this farm and the original house still stands, although the barn is a replacement built in 1926. The Lotenvitz corn crib is at the right.

storage. But it was not visited often and taking a broom as a defense against spider webs, mice, and garter snakes was not a bad idea. Of course, if you had a resident snake in the cellar, you usually did not have bugs or mice. Creepies or crawlies, the choice was yours.

The LPG Tank

While most of the farm buildings in the barnyard have a certain degree of charm, there is nothing interesting or decorative about the LPG tank. And all of the morning glories or hollyhocks available can't disguise its shape.

The introduction of LPG (liquefied petroleum gas) offered farmers a clean, inexpensive alternative to heating and cooking with wood. Most of the farmers had a big silver or white metal tank in their yard, holding a year's supply of gas. LPG became available for a number of farm applications in the 1930s. It was even possible to fuel your farm tractor using an LPG system. But the most efficient use for the system in the long run has been for home heating and cooking.

The Outhouse

It's the great equalizing experience for old and young, male and female, master and servant—using the outhouse. Nature's call has to be answered by both man and his beast. Although quickly disappearing from the landscape, the outhouse is the structure, along with the rural mailbox, that still identifies the farm as extremely rural. And using an outhouse is one of the experiences that defines and shapes a rural attitude.

Even after World War II, farms that were up to date (we didn't say modern) enough to have the convenience of indoor running water and a radio, still had an outhouse. The farm wife had indoor running water at her kitchen sink, even though she had to pump it from a well or cistern under the house, before she had the comfort of an indoor toilet.

Bathroom accommodations varied widely on the farms I visited in my youth. We had indoor plumbing on grandma's farm, an unusually large and comfortable bathroom downstairs that had been built as an addition on the back of the house. It had an outside entrance, which made it very convenient to wash up when you were really filthy from some farmyard chore. There was only one bathroom and there was no shower. But water was so scarce that very little water was ever poured in the tub.

The Country Gentleman, 1917.

Washing up meant scrubbing your face and hands. Water was precious so bathing was done out of extreme necessity rather than by routine. My grandmother had been trained as a nurse and had worked during the dreadful influenza epidemic of World War I so she closely monitored personal hygiene. Still, bath water and wash water went on the garden when we were finished and we were expected to share the basin with other family members when washing up before dinner.

If one grandmother was a stickler for cleanliness, the other was a lot more casual. The accommodations at their rural vacation place were primitive to city slickers like us but were normal for that part of central Missouri. The house was originally a Victory school, a one-room schoolhouse built before 1920 (and named to commemorate American efforts in World War I), like hundreds of others around middle-America. The original outhouse was gone, but its replacement was new and substantial, built about 60 feet from the front door. There was no water; we bought it from a neighbor and lugged it around in five-gallon containers.

Water became relatively convenient when a new well was finally dug. The well was near the porch, so my grandfather thoughtfully extended the porch floor and built a platform and a winch over the opening. Now grandma did not have to carry water up the stairs. There was electricity so he rigged

Pacific Rural Press, 1887.

COPY OF LETTER

FROM OUR

SACRAMENTO BRANCH:

SACRAMENTO, Dec. 5, 1887.

"Brown informs me that the Cyclone stood the terrible gale of last week better than any mill around Davisville, and that several mills, mostly of Eastern make, blew down, and just on account of the Cyclone doing so well, he has sold two more 12-foot mills, which I shipped him yesterday."

Send for

Illustrated

Catalogue

And Address of

Nearest

Local Agent.

a device that would winch the water bucket up the 100 feet or so from the water level. Now we had water for cooking, dishes, and washing, but what we had was used sparingly. But hey, we were on vacation anyway, so why bother with baths or laundry?

Outhouses were for sissies. Real men retired to a private place behind the barn or in a nearby woods—or so we were told. Given the number of critters taking shelter in the outhouse, I always felt that the sissies were pretty brave, especially at night. Even taking a flashlight along was not always a good idea; lots of bugs liked the light.

The relationship between human waste and disease had been scientifically demonstrated by 1850, according to the history books. By the turn of the century there was widespread understanding about the need to dispose of human waste in order to prevent infection. Many felt, however, that vapors or odors themselves were responsible for spreading cholera and other diseases. The thought was that if you couldn't smell it, it wasn't a problem.

Using the woods was convenient and traditional if you were out plowing in the back 40. If horse droppings were being added to a freshly turned furrow, why not a little human contribution as well? After all, it was a long, long walk back to the house.

Outhouses were a haven for all sorts of bugs and vermin, and the well-equipped outhouse came with a fly swatter and a broom. A bucket of corncobs and an outdated "Monkey" Ward catalog were also present in the little house on poor farms. Jokesters like to mention the necessity of using corncobs and pages from the Montgomery Ward catalog in the days when folks were too poor to afford toilet paper. (Yes, toilet paper was invented more than a century ago, and it looked pretty much like it does now.) The expression "as rough as a cob" takes on a completely new under-

The windmill was the technology that opened the West for settlement. Water is a farmer's most precious asset; it's impossible to raise livestock or grow a crop without adequate clean water. Wind power provided enough energy to pump water from a well to a cistern or other type of holding tank. Without a well and windmill, arid areas of western Kansas and Oklahoma could not have supported any agricultural activity. This carefully restored windmill appears in the collection of the county museum of Strasberg, Colorado.

Windmills are still commonly used to pump water for cattle in areas where it is too remote or too expensive to power a pump with electricity. *Ritzville Public Library Collection*

standing to those poor unfortunates who found themselves in the outhouse with nothing else at hand.

Modern indoor plumbing fixtures in the farmhouse are evident to the eye, but the most important part of the system is invisible. Most farms have a septic system underground to clean the waste from household water that goes down the drain. Water

testing and well testing are two important rural services, and that beautiful flower garden in a generous stretch of backyard may be the result of sowing some seeds over the septic tank.

Farm humor frequently includes some amusing stories about outhouses. There are numerous stories about outhouse adventures such as outhouses

The root cellar was a good storage place for all kinds of canned goods. Many cellars were spacious with whitewashed walls, shelving, emergency lighting and other essentials. Since the entire family sometimes had to spend several hours in the cellar waiting out a violent storm, there were usually a few amenities like coloring books and a pinochle deck. *John Vachon photo, Library of Congress, FSA*

catching on fire, and outhouses tipping over or being tipped over. Halloween pranksters especially liked to steal a local outhouse and relocate it to some highly visible place in the community like the roof of the local high school or the courthouse lawn. It was even more amusing if the outhouse had an unsuspecting occupant.

And of course some outhouses were more primitive than others. In cosmopolitan Independence, Missouri, it was a misdemeanor to build a privy

The Country Gentleman, 1916.

without a pit as early as the 1860s. But Agnes Bird provides a different personal experience from her childhood in rural Oklahoma, where the owner did not provide a pit, just the most minimal shack necessary for privacy. Located out in the farmyard, the privy shed provided a seat, but the rear of the shed was open to the elements. Unsuspecting occupants sometimes got pecked by a passing chicken.

One of the myths and mysteries of rural life is the legend of Chick Sale. A rural humorist with extraordinary word-of-mouth fame, his name lives as the synonym for outhouse. For many years I heard outhouses referred to as a "Chick Sale" without ever realizing that this curious label was really the name of a person.

While researching the topic of rural privies I questioned several sources, "Why do you call it a 'chick sale'," and the response was always unsatisfying, "Because that's what it's called!" The dictionary was no help; neither was the encyclopedia. My favorite reference librarian knew the term but was unable to locate authoritative source material. In desperation I consulted my personal oracle, my father. And my oracle provided some direction: Chick Sale was a person, he had a comic monologue, and he used to perform at county fairs and other gatherings.

Subsequent research has proven fruitless. I have yet to meet anyone who has actually heard his monologue about building the Deluxe, Top-of-the-line, Four-hole privy, so proof of Chick Sale's existence is hard to verify. Even now he seems to be a mythic figure—everybody knows his name, but

nobody knows where he was born. So if you hear an old-timer refer to his outhouse as a "Chick Sale 57," presume they are bragging about their superior accommodations and want some adulation.

Hired Hands: Human Versus Mechanical

The guidance in *Farm Knowledge*, my old copy of a farmer's handbook printed by Sears Roebuck in 1918, is very specific: "Transient laborers are as a class undesirable citizens." On specialized wheat farms, for example, the demand for labor in the harvest and threshing season is much greater than at any other season of the year. The specialized wheat farm that is large enough to use family labor during the remainder of the year cannot be operated without extra labor to bring in the crop.

This handbook on farm management, goes on to say "the most successful farm organization is found

where the farmer and his family do all the work. And
the least successful system of farming in the United
States is the operation of a farm by a farm manager."
While there is frequent debate about whether farmers were driven off their farms by mechanized farming and big business, there is ample consensus in the
old farm magazines about the difficulty of finding
any kind of help at any price.

It is doubtful that any of the farmers from the
Ohio Valley on west ever had the luxury of reliable
hired help. An article from *The Country Gentleman*
of November 1916 complains about the problem:
"A prosperous local dairy farmer commented on
the fact that he was not pushing his work very fast
by saying, 'My hired man is off, but the boy and I
are trying to do the best we can.' Then he point-
ed to the hay loader and remarked: 'There is
some satisfaction in having one hired man who
does not go off.'"

The magazine observes that another device
that is rapidly coming into use on the larger
farms is the hay hoist run by gasoline power.
With three wagons, two good teams can haul as
fast as a hay loader will load, and two men at the
barn can tend the hoist and the hay fork and
mow away, until the barn is pretty well filled.

Besides a powered hay hoist, farmers
were turning to powered milking machines.
In a highly specialized dairy region it was difficult to keep the full quota of help the year-
round. This was especially true where summer dairy-
ing was practiced. Many farmers kept 25 to 30 cows

The Country Gentleman, 1916.

Farm hands could earn good pay. But even during the Depression when work was scarce, good farm hands were hard to find. The Acme Employment agency in Minneapolis, Minnesota, was searching for a few good hands in 1939. *John Vachon photo, Library of Congress FSA*

and could get along well with one hired man and the wife to help milk. But the magazine notes that it was difficult to get the one man. And this shortage persisted before the manpower shortages of World War I and in an era when immigration was very high.

The writer notes that a milking machine is a good solution. He estimates that a hired man will cost $240 for eight months, and feeding him will take another $100. A well-equipped milking machine, including a small gasoline engine, can be

RIGHT

The hired hand—this one is rolling his own cigarette from a little bag of Bull Durham or some other tobacco. The farm wife was usually responsible for providing bed and board for the hired help, and since hired men frequently slept in the bunk house or barn and reportedly ignored regular bathing, the cumulative effect must have been stunning. Friends have told me that their hired man provided instruction in spitting, whittling, and tying knots, more reasons the farm wife was reluctant to include the hired man in the family circle. *The Kansas State Historical Society*

Agricultural self-sufficiency means that many farmers have their own fuel pump located near the barn. This venerable Texaco pump still sees daily service on Doug Peltzer's farm in Southern California.

installed for less than $400. And the housewife would often prefer to help run the milking machine than cook and clean for the hired hand.

Holding it All Together: Yankee Ingenuity at Work

The self-sufficient farmer had to be reasonably competent in several trades and it helped if mechanics

was one of them. Farmers were expected to know a little about veterinary science, some harness making, a little carpentry and blacksmithing as well as all the basics of plowing and planting. It was a lot to ask from a person with a fourth-grade education, but if the farmer lived in a supportive community, there was usually a specialist or two in the neighborhood when he needed help. The average farmer needed to be a reasonably competent general mechanic, and the term "shade tree" mechanic probably had its origin on the farm.

Independence and isolation stood alongside necessity as the mothers of invention. Most old-time farmers I knew could repair more with their bare hands and six inches of baling wire than today's farmer with a motorized lift and a full set of socket wrenches. Farmers recycled everything. But the two items that were recycled most often for those little short-term patches were baling wire and binder twine.

Baling wire and twine were carried in the farmer's pockets as he went around the barnyard doing the chores. They rode along in his coveralls with other bits of debris: old rusty nails, bolts, or nuts that were picked up in the pasture, pieces of barbed wire, chunks of chain, or an occasional harness buckle. Farmers tended to pick up bits and pieces when they saw them because stray chunks of metal could do serious damage or injury to farm animals and machinery. Finding a bolt or nut lying out in the field usually meant that something was loose and ready to fall off the cultivator you rode through here yesterday. But reaching in your pocket for a bit of baling wire was a good way to make that temporary fix on a gate latch until you could get around to doing a proper repair. Something always needed mending.

Coffee cans were the preferred containers for all sorts of little bits of repair items. I suppose there may have been a tidy soul who kept the lids on his coffee

cans, but I never met him. Coffee cans were opened with a funny little slotted key that was attached to the top of the can. They had to be opened carefully; the edges were razor sharp. Once the coffee was gone, a coffee can was the best device for all sorts of farm chores. You could use it for a feed scoop. It made a terrific drip catcher when wired under a faucet. The possibilities were endless.

There were no plastics in my youth. There were no broken bottles or aluminum soda cans lying around the farmyard, either. Any container that was not used to preserve food was carefully recycled for another use. Recycling was a way of life, not a lifestyle. Old buckets, enamelware from the kitchen, or discarded saucepans found a new barnyard use. Metal cans such as tin cans were only used for very short-term projects like holding fishing worms or starting seedlings, since tin cans from the store would rust and disintegrate.

There were two varieties of glass jars that appeared on the farm, but glass was not used around the barnyard because it was a danger to animals if it broke. Jars on the farm were either heavy glass jars used for canning or old mustard and mayonnaise jars. Glass jars belonged in the kitchen, not in the shop. Mason jars were used in pressure cooking; others were reused for jam and jelly.

Most farmers are aware that the Big Four of agricultural engineering, Cyrus McCormick, John Deere, J.I. Case, and John Deering, all were once barnyard mechanics. Henry Ford was another farm boy who preferred mechanics. So were dozens of inventors. Tinkering with farm machinery was both a creative outlet and an intellectual challenge.

Early tractor builders and designers were aware that farmers had to have machines that were easy to repair in the field with whatever tools the farmer might have at hand. But the builders also knew that most farmers would try to modify or improve any equipment they owned. So from World War I until the introduction of diesel tractors in the mid-1950s, the tractor manufacturers tried to build their machines simple and solid.

So most farmers had a shop or a tool bench, and many of them had a forge for a little blacksmithing. While none of them could shoe a horse, all of them had a plowshare or a cultivator tooth that needed straightening from time to time. "What— take half a day to go to town just to spend six bits on a replacement?" a farmer would typically say. "Well, I can take care of that myself in about 15 minutes." And they usually could and did.

Chores kept the farmer busy, and when he was finished with his own work, there was always something else that needed urgent attention. In this case the road to town needed to be cleared. So the farmer has fashioned this snowplow, apparently securing it to a clod buster. *Halbe Collection, The Kansas State Historical Society*

CHAPTER FOUR
The Barn and the Silo

Why Are Barns Painted Red?

It's just not a real farm without a barn. Drive along Interstate 35 down the middle of Iowa. Follow the gravel roads of Holmes County, Ohio. Over the hill, across the field, off in the distance, in a grove of trees, there's the tidiest little barn and silo you have ever seen. "Now we're really in the country," you say to yourself.

I confess that while I no longer wish for farm life, I am still overcome with recurrences of a condition that I can only describe as barn envy. I am drawn to barns by some deep emotion that I can identify but cannot label. There is a little file in my head, full of observations about the barns we see as we travel the countryside.

You used to be able to tell what part of the country you were in by the shape and color of the barns. In parts of northern Ohio the farmer puts his name and the age of his farm on his barn. In the eastern Ohio counties many of the barns

Horsepower was still in widespread use even as late as 1937. In this case it's being used to deliver a load of alfalfa to this McCormick thresher being used as an elevator near Little Fork, Minnesota. *Russell Lee photo, Library of Congress, FSA*

Some farmers proudly put their names on their barns; D. W. Snavely of Holmes County, Ohio, has his name on the roof, along with the year of construction, 1889. This barn serves several functions; the generous hayloft stores hundreds of tons of hay, horses are stabled on one side of the barn, and the other side of the barn has a small milking parlor and feed area for the family milk cows. This barn was apparently first built to served mixed farming, a family farm that grew corn as a cash crop, used horses for power, grew hay to feed the horses, and kept a couple of cows and a pig or two to feed the family.

are 150 years old, dating to before the Civil War. They have lacy woodwork detailing on shuttered windows. Is the barn red? Then you're probably in Iowa. And if you see huge white barns with stone foundations, then you may be looking at Wisconsin dairy barns.

Farmers on the West Coast tend to leave their barns unpainted. Built of rot-resistant redwood, the barns in California, Oregon, and Washington are weathered to a silver-gray. To a Midwesterner these barns look like they need paint. Nothing makes a farm look more prosperous than a freshly painted

Lacey window and shutter detail from the Snavely barn. White barns with lacy window treatment can be found on dozens of barns in this part of northeastern Ohio; it seems to be a local tradition.

The Country Gentleman, 1916.

barn. The farm house can be snug and clean, but a neglected barn is a bad sign.

Barns come in all sizes and shapes, round barns, square barns, and barns with fading advertisements painted on the side. Some barns have gambrel roofs, the shape we call a "barn roof." Some barns have enormous haylofts, and some are built with sheds on the side.

What kind of barn is it? Was it built as a dairy barn with a milking parlor and a cooling room to chill milk and sanitize the cans? Is it a general-purpose barn with stalls for horses, a tack room, and a generous hayloft? Were the cows kept in the building on the side? What shape is the roof? Does the roof come to a point, topped with a lightning rod or a weather vane?

Why are barns painted red in some parts of the country and painted white elsewhere? There doesn't seem to be one simple and satisfying answer; the reason seems to be part of farm folklore. The best answer seems to be that the choice of color is partly

This relatively small barn in northern Missouri is painted red, the most common local color for barns in this area. Here the farms are small, corn and soybeans are the cash crops, and most farms were established after tractors were introduced. This barn is interesting because there seems to be no fences or paddocks; the barn functions as a garage.

due to local custom and partly due to the expense of painting a barn. The selection of red was due both to the low cost of the iron-oxide pigment used to color red paint, and to the fact that there were really just a few pigments in existence.

Paint has a simple recipe with only three or four ingredients. It's made up of a pigment or color mixed with enough linseed oil and turpentine to make it soupy enough to apply with a brush.

Sometimes a fourth ingredient is added to help the mixture dry a little faster. Colors usually available for barns were ochre (a mustard yellow) or iron-oxide red. Blue and green pigments were expensive and tended to fade. Since the longest-lasting pigment was iron oxide—the rusty red we see on most barns—red was the logical choice. Red had the additional advantage of hiding the inevitable dirt from animals and farm machinery.

That's not to say that all barns are painted red. Quite a few of them are white, usually painted at the same time the farmhouses were painted. Again, the availability of the pigment contributes to the cost, and the least-expensive pigment was white lead. The second choice was white made with white lead and zinc oxide combined and mixed with linseed oil and a dryer.

Whitewash, another option, was cheaper than real paint but it had some drawbacks, so it was usually reserved for buildings that were going to need to be painted or coated every year or so anyway. Whitewash provided a thin coating and it was stinky, not suitable for indoor use. There were several recipes to make white-

Corporate headquarters for agricultural Americans, the farmstead with its barn and outbuildings shelters that important business institution: the family farm. Farms are now a venture that is operated with tremendous efficiency. Less than 2 per-cent of the American population is now classified as farmers, yet they manage to feed the rest of us.

The Country Gentleman, 1927.

wash, but it usually combined lime, water, and milk or casein. Unfortunately, these latter two ingredients made whitewash smell like very bad milk.

The chicken coop usually got an annual coat of whitewash; so did fences and the cellar. Whitewash was thin and runny so it didn't have

Barn Shops And Bone Piles

Farmers are mechanics—always have been and probably always will so remain. One hundred years ago they had to learn to assemble, adjust, and repair plows, planters, cultivators, drills, threshing machines, feed mills, and more, all horse-powered. Then along came the tractor, a balky steed at first, with a whole new set of gastrointestinal problems to puzzle out and correct.

The dusty loft or storeroom of an old barn can accommodate more neglected treasures than any old attic. Ancient cream separators, old tools, bits of tack and harness, a century-old buggy, and if you're very lucky, you might just discover most of a semi-operational steam engine or thrasher.

You can't have a farm without a shop, and that shop will likely be in one of the barns or a dedicated machine building. In fact, many farms have multiple shops designed for different functions. Our friends the Kosters have a dedicated building for equipment repair. It has been in use since shortly after the Koster family homesteaded their spread back in 1880, and some of the tools in the shop look original. There is still a forge, anvil, and blacksmith tools in shop, and they still get used. Cliff and Billy Koster don't have to rebuild wooden wagon wheels anymore, so those specialized tools have disappeared, but I've seen them in other shops in Ohio where horse-drawn vehicles are still an important form of transportation.

The Kosters keep and use farm machines until the wheels fall off, then they stash the derelict parts in the barn. But as long as a machine can pull its own weight and there's a job it can do, you will find it in the field. The Kosters still thresh their soybeans with a bean harvester built in 1942 and modified and repaired in dozens of places. But it works, brings in the beans, and avoids the cost of a custom harvester. That's one way the Kosters have kept their farm in the black while others with modern equipment (and the debt that goes with it) have gone broke and lost their farms. The farm shop keeps the old machines going.

Every farm shop has a "possibles" pile outside and most have some machinery that won't work again but is kept for sentimental reasons. One of those sentimental reasons is that the equipment is paid for, and the farmer can't stand the idea of throwing away that old John Deere B just because it's got a cracked block. You can fix a cracked block, sometimes, and there are folks around who will sell you a used one, so the tractor gets tucked into the back of the barn where it will stay for 50 years.

Sometimes these things actually get recycled. Cliff converted a 1965 Dodge Dart into a tree shaker, grafting the shaker from one old machine onto the chassis and running gear of one very old, bombed-out, car. It is the damnedest looking thing you've ever seen, but it works and it's paid for.

If anybody ever dusts off the stuff in Cliff's barns and shops, you could call it a museum and charge admission. There's a huge 1914 Harris harvester in there, a couple of buggies, harnesses, and hitches for the mules that were sold 80 years ago. A big, 1925 Caterpillar tractor is in one of the barns, along with a Case windrower from the 1950s, a small fleet of old cars, and a huge Holt engine that once powered a grain combine. A header wagon, unused for half a century, is still there, too.

Few farmers are immune to the collecting bug. Many cherish the tools that their ancestors used to farm, keeping them out of love and frugality. Jacob Yoder is an Amish farmer in Holmes County, Ohio. His ancient horse barn contains a sturdy old wagon, stashed back of the haymow and the grain bins. Jacob noticed me examining the wagon, long since retired from service. "One of these days I'm gonna get me some paint and restore that thing," he said. Barn shops and bone piles—it's an American farm tradition, even with the Amish.

It's a cold and snowy morning in eastern Washington state and the horses need breakfast. In really cold weather horses would be kept inside the barn, so seeing them outside like this is an indication that the weather was not too severe. Large teams, sometimes as many as 30 head of horses and mules were used to pull the giant combines in eastern Washington. Large farms required a lot of horsepower. Tractors were a welcome improvement; you could park them for a week and walk away. *Ritzville Public Library*

the covering power of real paint. But since you were using a new coat every year or so, fading was not a problem.

The barn on my grandparents' farm was an enormous disappointment. In fact, it was worse than disappointing; it was an embarrassment—it wasn't even a real barn. The original house and barn had been built in the 1870s. The house had been renovated, but the original barn had never been repaired. Leaning and dangerous, it sheltered only a rusting hay rake. Eventually it was razed and not replaced. While we had a corn crib

"As big as a barn door" is the old expression . . . well, how big is that? For early farmers, the barn doors needed to be large enough to drive a pair of horses through. When farmers started driving tractors, barn doors changed.

LEFT
A farmer near Little Fork, Minnesota, takes a pinch of snuff. He is wearing the typical farm work uniform of blue denim bib coveralls. The leather cord disappearing inside his bib secures his pocket watch. If a farmer had a watch at all, it was usually a pocket watch, carried on a strap. Wristwatches could get caught in farm machinery and were for "city folks." *Russell Lee photo, Library of Congress, FSA*

Making water run uphill

It is in the records made by General Electric motors over long periods of hard usage that the results of careful testing and skilled workmanship are found. Not only in pumping stations, but in cement plants, on street railways, and in steel mills, General Electric motors are proving their worthiness to bear the G-E monogram. The General Electric Company manufactures many electrical products which are used on the farm. The G-E Farm Book describing these products may be obtained from your local light and power company.

IN arid regions of the world, water is one of the precious commodities. And within the memory of nearly every farmer there have been short seasons of drought and withering heat that have brought home to him the value of his water supply.

In California where thousands of square miles of luxurious vegetation bear witness to the infinite resourcefulness of engineering, you will find electric motors running night and day sometimes for six months at a time, pumping the water needed for irrigation. But irrigation is not the only purpose for which electricity makes water "run uphill." Running water in the kitchen, a modern bathroom, and a liberal supply of fresh water for stock are no longer considered luxuries on any farm, where electricity is available.

The instant dependable power of the electric motor does not need to be tended or supervised. Such are the economy and simplicity of its operation, and the advantages of distant and automatic control, that electric motors are supplanting all other kinds of power apparatus wherever there is work to be done.

The Country Gentleman, 1926.

Barns provide wonderful space to store old farm equipment like this wagon. Storage spaces such as these are part of the reason that so many farm implements have survived. Protected by the weather, threshers, wagons, and tractors remain in surprisingly good condition after decades of neglect.

and a chicken house and a smokehouse, there was no silo. So you can see why I still occasionally suffer from barn envy. It's probably an incurable emotional condition, brought on by early barn and silo deprivation.

The Silo Full of Milo

Soybeans, millet, sudan, milo
All are good to fill the silo.

Standing next to the barn, the silo is the farm structure that has the most characteristic silhouette on the horizon. It's interesting to note that the silo, that wonderful invention that has contributed so much to successful and profitable agriculture, was an American invention. The first American silo was built in 1873, according to historian Wayne D. Rasmussen. It was developed to allow better winter feeding of dairy cattle. The

The Functional Barn

The barn is perhaps the most pure, unpretentious form of architecture. Nowhere else does function determine form quite so religiously. While you'll sometimes find ornament and decoration on a barn, most are stark, clean, and elegant. They are designed to be part of a money-making operation. Every detail and element seems part of a grand plan with a pay-off, somewhere, sometime, somehow.

A stock barn, like Jacob Yoder's in Holmes County, Ohio, is a beautiful object, but everything about it is designed to be functional and durable. Its beauty is a happy accident.

The stock—draft horses and dairy cows—are accommodated on the ground level. They are the barn's *functional* foundation, the reason it exists. Both cows and horses are sociable animals, happy to have the company of their own kind. Box stalls, of sturdy construction, house each massive horse. The floor is concrete, for ease of cleaning, and padded with plenty of straw for comfortable footing. The stable area for the horses is fairly small, with stalls for six animals. The walls are concrete and rock, whitewashed. Just outside the stalls, along the alley that runs from one end of the barn to the other, hang the collars and harness for each horse. A watering trough of concrete construction stands to the right of the barn door.

Overhead, and not by much, are the floor beams for the granary floor and haymow. These beams are old—Jacob doesn't know how old, but suspects they, and the basic barn, have served over 100 years. These beams are very characteristic of old barns, obviously hand-hewn and with the bark still on the sides. Each beam seems generously perforated with insect holes, but there isn't any sagging. Whitewash covers all the exposed surfaces.

Above the horses is a large haymow and granary; it is a simple matter, thanks to the design of the barn, to pass the hay and grain down to the stock below. Both levels are accessible to wheeled vehicles, thanks to careful placement of the barn, plus a ramp up to the second level.

The Yoder barn, like thousands of others across the country, is constructed with timber framing techniques. Instead of a multitude of straight, standard 2x4s and the larger lumber used today, the barn builders of the past went out in the back lot and selected their timber. After felling and seasoning, the lumber was hauled to the site for dressing and fitting. As with the Yoder barn, these timbers sometimes got very little attention before getting installed in place, complete with bark.

Many of these barns use no metal fasteners in the framing at all. Instead, they are held together with artful, interlocking joints. The most common of these joints is the *mortise* (a hole in a timber) and *tenon* (a pin cut in the end of another timber), secured with wooden pins ("trunnels," an ancient word meaning *tree-nail*). Properly constructed, the mortise and tenon is a living, breathing joint of tremendous strength that will last far longer than conventional techniques. Wood simply doesn't rust, while spikes and bolts always do, sooner or later. Some New England barns are strong and sound 200 years after they were built.

In the West, such timber was seldom available and more conventional techniques were employed. A western barn built 100 years ago used mortise and tenon joints along with conventional fasteners. The basic material was redwood, cut and milled far away, and brought to the site by railroad and mule-drawn wagons. Even after a century of use, these structures are holding up well.

Western barns use a different form to serve the same function required of the Yoder stock barn. Western barns are long and fairly low, with one long row of stalls along each wall. A central alley serves both, with a big door at each end.

A tack room is a standard fixture in western horse barns, a wonderful place if you like the smells of leather, horse sweat, and saddle soap. It is always at the end of the barn, by the door nearest the yard, with pegs and racks for the heavy collars, hames, harnesses, and hitches—along with the ghosts of long-gone horses, mules, teamsters, and muleskinners.

The interior of this Ohio barn indicates the degree of engineering and craftsmanship in barn construction that was possible more than a century ago. It is possible that the farmer used timbers from his own farm, cutting and shaping with an adz, smoothing the beams only if necessary.

Barn heaven. Imagine a barn big enough to hold scores of horses downstairs and dozens of cowboys in the bunkhouse upstairs. Imagine a bunkhouse fireplace so large that whole logs were hoisted through the haymow to warm the ranch hands. Built of redwood and painted white, this barn was built in California's Central Valley for a cattle ranch that covered thousands of acres.

Indiana Silo Company of Anderson, Indiana, is sometimes credited with developing the first silo. And if that claim cannot be justified, then surely the company's marketing efforts on behalf of silage qualifies it for immortality.

In 1910 the Indiana Silo Company printed a little book entitled "Silo Profits," composed entirely of 200 glowing letters from farmers praising the profits of silos. Farmer O. F. Peterson

"What you got there, John?"

"Some war paint for the old barn."

"Didn't know your barn was a fighter!"

"You bet she is! The life of any barn is just one scrap after another—with the weather! In the winter it's snow and frost and sleet. In summer it's wind and sun and rain. Just now my barn's yelling for help— and here's the stuff that will give her the best of it for a long time to come."

"What kind of paint is it?"

"*Sherwin-Williams Commonwealth Barn Red*. Those

The Country Gentleman, 1915.

from Zion City, Illinois, writes a typical letter. "How nice it is to sit in the house in the rocker and see my neighbor out in the field with a shovel and an ax, digging in two or three feet of snow and the sweat running down his face and puffing like a steam engine. There is where the Indiana Silo comes in for comfort, and the next thing the manure is in fine shape to go back on the land."

What is a silo and how does it work? A silo is an oversized can of cow chow. It looks like a round tower, made of wood or concrete and as airtight as possible. Farmers cut and chop corn or alfalfa or milo or a mixture, and load it in the silo to keep it

LEFT

Stock such as horses, cows, and sometimes sheep and goats are housed on the lowest levels of the barn. The hay for the horse is on top of the barn in the mow and it's pitch-forked down into the stall for bedding or for feed. Then after the horse processes the hay, the stalls are "mucked out" and piles of manure are scooped over to the side of the barnyard to age.

away from light and air. Traditionally, farmers were always trying to find a nourishing food for their livestock that was inexpensive and easy to grow locally. Old farm magazines all carry articles and discussions on feed in practically every issue. When farmers discovered that some crops would stay green and fresh all winter if they were stored in silos, farm production took a quantum leap.

An article in the *Farm Journal* from September 1937 has a few specific opinions about silage. "King of the silage crops is corn. The silo is becoming, however, more than a competitor of the corn crib. It is asking the haymow to come out and fight. In Michigan this summer, where rain has hindered haying, farmers are putting their alfalfa into silos. Molasses is added to the alfalfa to supply the lactic acid necessary to make it keep." Other legumes and grasses, as well as small grain crops, can be used for silage in the same way.

The secret of the preservation of silage is the acid content of the green plant. Most green plants preserve well if they contain enough sugar to produce the acid needed.

The Country Gentleman, 1915.

Corn, sorghum, and milo have enough sugar but alfalfa, soybeans, and wheat do not. So farmers mix them, tossing them together like a salad that makes its own dressing. Silage is preserved because the acids "pickle" the greens. It's coleslaw for cows and they love it.

The classic barn. This barn has a gambrel or "barn" roof and the stalls for the livestock on the first floor. This barn, near Charles City, Iowa, has been in continuous use for 70 years.

Silos were one of the earliest farm "inventions" that allowed the farmer to accumulate wealth since it let the farmer keep his livestock over the winter. Providing an adequate supply of food, the silo helped the farmer to nourish his prize horses or a dairy herd through the winter months when pasture was not available and the cost of hay was prohibitive. *Howard Ande photo*

When the tractor replaced the horse, barns became a garage for the new, expensive mechanized equipment that was becoming the farmer's best friend. More than one farmer "modified" the barn door when he forgot that the tractor and its implements were taller and wider than the old horse and wagon. *Howard Ande photo*

Silage solved an enormous problem for farmers: what to feed their livestock through the winter. Silage allowed dairy farmers to build and maintain their stock over several years without having to drastically reduce their herds every fall. It meant that the investment in high-quality breeding stock of any type could pay off, since farmers could now afford to keep a good animal when the pastures were covered with snow. And since a crop could be trucked in and chopped for silage, a farmer was no longer completely dependent on local pastures and weather for fodder.

The introduction and widespread use of silage in farm production changed American menus. Using silage meant that meat became available to American markets all year around. Beef production was no longer restricted by the seasons, and both the price and production of beef cattle could now be controlled. The use of silage is one of the most important developments in American agriculture.

We're used to seeing the big custom threshing machines in the field, separating the kernels from the straw. But putting a small thresher inside the barn makes good sense too. It keeps the crew out of the rain or sun or wind and allows the thresherman a little more time to process the harvest. This Dion is probably the best "barn-size" thresher still available.

While the shape and size of the barn has a great deal in common with similar buildings in Europe, there is something distinctly American about a big, red barn in a field. Like the eagle and apple pie, the image of a barn recalls our farm history.

CHAPTER FIVE

The Pasture and the Field

After the barn and house, the most important farm feature is the pasture. It should be covered with lush Kentucky bluegrass, be surrounded by a freshly painted white fence, and have a few magnificent shady trees right next to a little pond.

On our farm the fence was barbed wire, the grass always seemed patchy, and the trees were part of the fence line. We picked our path cautiously when visiting the stock pond. The slimy pond always had frogs and fish, but it was as close to a swimming pool as we could get on hot summer days. Walking through the pasture meant keeping an eye out for two things: cows and cow manure. While the cows were usually tolerant of people in their pasture, every now and again they were known to get cranky. Cow manure was another story. Cow pies were a common hazard, although most of them were dried out and relatively odor free.

Eastern Washington was wheat country, and the rolling acres were harvested by crews like this one, operating a pair of horse-drawn Harris harvesters. Dozens of horses and men were needed to bring in the crop; hard, hot work for the crews and the farm wives back in the kitchen getting dinner ready. *Ritzville Public Library*

Abundance: wheat, corn, more wheat, and timber. The fertile farmland near Fergus Falls, Minnesota, around World War II.
Marion Post Wolcott photo, Library of Congress, FSA

Some farmers still do it the old way; Jacob Yoder and sons bring in a load of Ohio hay.

And a dried cow pie was always a good weapon to toss at the unwary.

Pasture and Forage—Wonder Grass

A hundred years ago the prairies were covered with native grasses. As farmers moved onto the land, native grasses were quickly replaced with forage crops and cash crops such as corn and wheat. Interestingly, two of our most widely cultivated crops, alfalfa and soybeans, are not even native to America. Soybeans were introduced from Japan; alfalfa came from Chile.

After hard lessons were learned, one native grass was rediscovered and reintroduced. After the Dust Bowl years of the '30s, efforts were made to plant buffalo grass (grama grass) as a cover crop to keep precious topsoil in place.

Our agricultural mistakes have caused some hard economic lessons. Today's farmer takes a careful look at his soil and the local conditions. He plans before he plants. We have learned that parts of the prairie should never be cultivated. And we have learned that irrigation is not always a good idea, even when the soil is fertile. Farmers are taking another look at buffalo grass and other wild plant species, carefully replacing the prairie ecosystems, and using native plants to complement their cultivated fields.

Osage Oranges and Barbed Wire

Osage orange trees, discovered on the Osage River of Arkansas, can now be found all over Illinois and the Great Plains. The fruit is a light lime green in color with a pebbled skin like a navel orange and about the size of a grapefruit. Mature hedgerows line fields all over Missouri, Kansas, and the rest of the Midwest, and the plant, once

This quartet of horses is waiting for a ride. Mules were also widely used for farm chores and considered to be smarter and more reliable than horses. *Ritzville Public Library*

California farmers pioneered specialized agricultural equipment, and here are two examples. The Caterpillar tractor, a tracked crawler for loamy soils, and the Bean fruit sprayer were both designed in the Golden State. The two companies that developed them, Caterpillar and FMC, are now both located in the Midwest. *San Jose Historical Museum*

cultivated by the thousands, is now considered a nuisance. The fruit is inedible and the wood is too dense to use for lumber.

Cattle sometimes get the fruit lodged in their throats and can suffocate. Cattle farmer Orrin Long says that his cattle just eat them like apples during the summer. The only time they cause a problem is in the winter when the fruit is frozen and large chunks get stuck. But Long likes Osage oranges for another reason: they still make a very useful hedgerow.

The Osage orange is a tough, shrubby tree that grows quickly, has enormous thorns, and resists drought. It suckers and spreads from the bottom. A row of trees planted as a hedge will quickly fill in and make an impenetrable barrier. It is very tough to harvest, but a persistent logger could probably get a fence post or two when the trees matured.

When you are a kid, however, Osage oranges are absolutely the best "hand grenades" for a juvenile game of "war." Usually too large to be thrown accurately by a child, they split apart with a satisfying mess if they hit something. In addition, they smell vile and split easily when slightly rotten, guaranteed to offend the opposing army as well as your mother.

The 1852 edition of *The Prairie Farmer* reports the introduction and development of the Osage orange as a hedge plant. Developed as a hedge by professor Jonathan Turner of Illinois College, in Jacksonville, Illinois, the plant was widely advertised as fencing material. Subsequent issues of the magazine praised its virtues, and many readers wrote to editor John S. Wright about their experience with the new plant.

The first patents on barbed wire were awarded to Joseph Glidden of Dekalb, Illinois, in 1874, but it was nearly a decade before large-scale production became practical. Poultry wire or chicken wire was an older development, first manufactured in England sometime in the 1840s. Farmers and stockmen had tried using various kinds of wire fencing but single strands of wire expanded during hot weather and broke easily.

Building a fence was time-consuming and back-breaking work if you had the materials at hand. It became an impossible chore if you were short of suitable wood. Farmers on the Great Plains had a serious problem: lumber was so scarce that they even built their houses of sod. Some early farmers tried fences of sod and there are even some fence posts in eastern Kansas that have been worked out of quarried limestone. But a limestone post still needed a cross member of wood or wire.

Midwestern farmers and nurserymen tried planting hedges of the Osage orange, and for a few

Len Bisco and family lined up for the photographer near Callaway, Nebraska. The Bisco house was small but solid with glass windows and wood siding—quite an improvement over the sod huts of some of their neighbors. There are three children—baby is sitting in the buggy—and even the horses are holding still for the photographer. *Solomon D. Butcher Collection, Nebraska State Historical Society*

years it seemed to be fairly satisfactory as a fencing alternative. Speculators foresaw a need for thousands of trees when the Homestead Act opened up the Great Plains in 1862. They stockpiled Osage orange seedlings and seeds to peddle to homesteading farmers, only to go bust when barbed wire became plentiful and cheap.

But Osage orange trees still have their uses. The wood is extremely resistant to insects and makes great fence posts if you cut it and install staples when it's still green. Cut back to the ground, the tree will sucker from the bottom, producing a bouquet of canes that quickly fills in and becomes a new hedge. It's self-renewing, an important resource for those who know how to manage it.

Soils from the Ground Up

The first thing you hear from your soils professor in an agriculture class is a very short definition of

Capper's Farmer,

the word soil. "Soil is *not* dirt. Dirt is something you find under your sofa. Soil is what you use to grow plants. You should have soil under your fingernails, not dirt." You quickly get the idea that soil is magical and should be treated with respect and affection. Or else.

It almost goes without saying that the two major factors that determine the kind of farm you can have are soil and climate. And you can't do much about either one. So if your heart is set on growing cotton, go south. If you want to raise racehorses, you are going to need bluegrass pasture, so that means Kentucky and Tennessee. It's the soil that determines whether you will pay $5,000 or 50 cents an acre for your farm. A barn and house can be rebuilt in a summer, but sometimes the soil has been ruined beyond salvage.

It was a surprise to me to learn that soil could be worn out and used up. America had a couple of soil crises that we heard about in the history classes. One was during the Depression, when the soil dried up and blew away, making farming impossible. The history classes were never really specific about why

LEFT
A team of Belgians cuts oats the same way it was done over a century ago in Holmes County, Ohio.

Hard Times

Farming is never an easy life. Hailstones or a tornado can destroy a crop and wipe out a year's work and a year's income in twenty minutes. While most of the history books talk about the Great Depression of the 1930s, the books fail to mention that it was really several depressions, each of them with its own set of circumstances, each needing a different solution. Then there were the drought, the locusts, and the dust storms. In a way, the economic depression was the easiest to handle.

Farmers were hardest hit in several areas, the wheat belt in Canada and the Oklahoma Dust Bowl. An economic depression, combined with several years of drought and then high winds, had killed crops and removed topsoil. There was no way that the land could recover. American farmers learned their lesson too late. They paid for a failure to plant cover crops and to practice contour plowing. One of the most graphic descriptions of what it was really like comes from the firsthand accounts in *Ten Lost Years*, a book about the drought and Depression in Canada:

The dust storms. Nobody is ever going to write truly what a dust storm was like. We had them; I've seen them when you couldn't see the front of your car. Millions of acres just blowing away from all through the American Midwest states and over toward the Dakotas and Minnesota, Wisconsin, up into Manitoba, Saskatchewan, and Alberta. Things we'll never forget, and they could come again.

First the heat comes in cycles, years apart but years together when it comes, and who the hell is to know? We didn't have all that much ground water and what we had we were using up; the water table was dropping. The Palliser Triangle shouldn't have ever been broken to the plough. We know that now. Grazing, stock. The buffalo thrived like a green bay tree on it and so could cattle. We had this loose sub-soil that had no holding power and then we had the winds. Why them winds came, I'm not sure anyone knew, but I've seen them blow for two weeks at a time, blowing hard. Blowing the goddamned country right out from under our feet and nothing we could do about it.

But grasshoppers. Trillions. They would black out the sky and when they passed, nothing would be left. I've seen an ordinary kitchen broom leaning up against the side of a granary where we were crushing oats and when the hoppers were finished, all that was left of that broom was the handle and you couldn't tell it had been a handle because it was so chewed up except for the metal band which kept the bristles held together. Grasshoppers didn't eat machinery, but by God, I've seen them eat the leather off the seat of a John Deere tractor.

LEFT
Soil Erosion near Tupelo, Mississippi, March 1936. Farming has changed, but these are the farm practices that contributed to the Depression and Dust Bowl conditions of the 1930s. Poor plowing practices without erosion control caused topsoil to wash away leaving deep gullies that were impossible to farm. The rich topsoil disappeared and the remaining material would support neither crop nor livestock. There was nothing to do but abandon the farm.
Walker Evans photo, Library of Congress, FSA

Locusts or grasshoppers, whatever you call them, will destroy a crop or anything else if they are hungry enough. Locusts hatch on a periodic schedule. The most devastating hatches take place every 17 years or so. This field of milo has been eaten down to stubs.

These small boys are lucky enough to have their own boat. The "Valiant" is being rowed on the irrigation canal below the C. B. Reynolds residence near Kearney, Nebraska, in 1904. Kearney was, and is, an important and prosperous community on the Platte River, the location of Fort Kearney, a stop along the famous Oregon Trail. *Solomon D. Butcher Collection, Nebraska State Historical Society*

things were so awful or how they got that way. Dorothea Lange's famous picture of the migrant mother and her two children illustrated the anguish without offering explanation.

There is another soil crisis going on now, as the best soil is covered by suburbs. City people assume that technology will take care of them. Farmers in many suburban areas have had to fight back with political campaigns to preserve the land. No-growth initiatives and recall elections are not the result of new housing-development issues; they are usually related to the limited availability of water and really good soil. Farmers know that technology is only a tool, like a tractor, and all the manure in the world cannot bring back a field once it has been used by a housing development.

From *Capper's Farmer*, 1950.

Crops

There are a few things that ought to be pretty obvious to most people, but nowadays it's pretty rare to find an average person who can identify corn when he sees it. Drive across the middle of Iowa; take Interstate 35 from Kansas City to St. Paul, and identify the crops growing along the side of the road. It's often difficult to tell the difference between oats, wheat, and barley; between corn and sorghum.

Here's the most important thing to remember about choosing farm real estate: location, location, location. It's that simple. You can get great corn in Iowa, Illinois, and Nebraska, but you can't grow oranges. All of the irrigation and fertilizer money can buy cannot make up the difference in the climate and the growing season. So if you meet a farmer in Missouri, you can pretty much bet he'll be growing corn and beans,

because that is what grows best in Missouri's soil and climate.

Wheat farming is now pretty much limited to the Great Plains of Canada, the Dakotas, Nebraska, and Kansas. And any real farmer who listens to the lyrics from the Broadway musical *Oklahoma!* laughs his socks off at the line, "the corn is as high as an elephant's eye." There's more corn in the musical than the state. Or how about being "as corny as Kansas in August"? Well, maybe eastern Kansas. Sure, corn will grow in Kansas and Oklahoma. But it grows better in Iowa and Illinois, and there's a good reason that Nebraska is known for its Cornhuskers.

Harvesting and Threshing

At the end of every growing season, once a year, was the harvest. It was the time of year that required extraordinary effort by the entire agricultural community. A farmer could plow and plant by himself, taking his own time to get the seed into the ground. And he could cultivate on his own. But harvesting required

This wins the Ugly Tractor award. It's a prototype, a good example of farm ingenuity, circa 1918. The loamy soil of valley orchards needed special implements and this machine was built to meet those requirements by the R. M. Lipe Machine Shop in Santa Clara Valley. *San Jose Historical Museum*

Threshers made the work easier when they were first introduced over a century ago, but they needed constant attention as the dozens of gears and belts required endless greasing and oiling for proper operation.

a community effort. Depending on the crop, harvesting and threshing required the effort of dozens of hired hands and all the neighbors.

Threshing probably required the most manpower. And it required the most womanpower to feed the manpower. All of the cereal and grain crops—wheat, oats, rye, and barley—required a coordinated effort: cutting the grain in the field, binding it into bundles, picking up the bundles of shocks in a wagon, and hauling them to a threshing

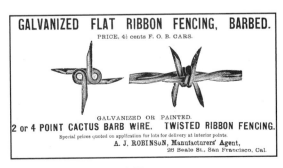

Pacific Rural Press, 1887.

Valley of the Heart's Delight was the name given to the fertile orchards of Northern California. Fertile soil and a magnificent climate, this enormously productive region provided much of the nation's plums, pears, prunes, and apricots as well as year round production of lettuce and row crop vegetables. *San Jose Historical Museum*

machine. The threshing machine removed the heads of grain from the stalk or straw and then deposited the straw in one pile and the precious grain in a funnel that led to a burlap bag.

In the early days of horse-drawn harvesters and threshers, it took a dozen men and scores of horses to harvest a crop. Since threshing activity began before dawn and went on all day, the farm wife was expected to provide breakfast, dinner, and supper for the crew. Some wives called in neighbors to help, since they barely had time to finish washing up the dishes from one meal before they had to start on another.

In many communities, the neighbors formed a threshing circle or ring, a group of neighbors that shared the expense of owning an expensive thresher. The neighbors provided the necessary manpower and womanpower to bring in the crop. Contrast this with today when the harvesting is done by one or two people, each driving a machine that harvests, threshes, weighs, and loads.

The Country Gentleman, 1917

farmer but a new way of using his time and effort. Mechanized equipment had been around for decades; the reaper and the thresher had been in use for 60 years. But lighter, more maneuverable tractors like the Hart-Parr offered farmers more flexibility and independence in managing crops. It made farming much more productive and profitable.

In the beginning it seems that tractor sales and acceptance started slowly. Most farmers were still using horse-drawn equipment or steam-driven equipment for plowing and planting. But success breeds competition, and soon dozens of mechanics were building their own experimental model

The Tractor

Steam-powered traction machines had been operating on large farms in Europe and America since the 1880s. But a couple of smart agricultural engineering students from the University of Wisconsin, Charles Hart and Charles Parr, built and tested the first gasoline tractor before 1900. They met at school, found they were both interested in tractors, and decided to work together. They designed and tested their machine before they graduated, putting their little machine into mass production in 1904. The word "tractor" itself was popularized by W. H. Williams, another University of Wisconsin classmate who became the Hart-Parr Company's sales manager.

"Power farming" was both a slogan and farm-management concept developed by an advertising copywriter before 1910. This concept appeared with the advent of the gasoline tractor, and it introduced not only new equipment to the

The Hunter family of Agnews, California, has come down to the irrigation ditch to see how the new pump is operating. Mr. Hunter has removed the back tire and is using the rear wheel to power the pump. Inventive farmers were always trying new ways to reduce labor and increase productivity and many farmers adapted their available equipment to their need. For example, many farmers about this time were buying conversion kits for their new Model T Ford autos, converting them for use as a small tractor. The picture was taken about 1912. *San Jose Historical Museum*

Ramie: A New Marvel Crop

It's easier to recall some of the successful crops such as alfalfa, soybeans, and grama grass and overlook some of the crops that have been less than successful. This article by Wheeler McMillan in the *Farm Journal* of March 1946 is a reminder that marvels can come—and go.

Down in the Florida Everglades a few weeks ago I saw growing on more than 1,000 acres what may be the most sensational new crop since the soybean. I saw another 1,000 acres or more of land being prepared for further plantings. The crop is *ramie* and the product is a fiber of amazing qualities. From perennial roots the nettlelike stalks shoot up four to seven feet. After cutting, more stalks promptly grow again, so that in two months or less another crop may be cut. Three crops a year, at least.

When woven with wool, ramie prevents shrinking. Ramie fabric absorbs perspiration and other moisture easily, dries quickly, washes well, resists mildew, and permits removal of most difficult stains. A man who was wearing what I took to be a new shirt told me it had been laundered 65 times. Ramie will grow in suitable soil where the frost reaches down less than two or three inches. Experimental fields can be seen in Texas, Alabama, and Georgia. Once planted, the stand is good for four years or more, until the roots choke up all the space between the rows. Good cultivating yields 500 to 800 pounds of fiber per acre.

Ramie is still around, easy to grow but as difficult as flax to process and weave. Like the Osage orange, the kudzu vine, the eucalyptus tree, and other historic "marvels," it is one of those plants that should probably not be cultivated as a crop.

tractor makers any more than it is the fault of the farmers. You may standardize the quality of your tractor to a superfine degree, but how about the standardization of the purchaser's ingenuity, skill, versatility, good or bad fortune in production?

Thanks to the small tractor the industry has already approached such standardization that it is possible for 32 makers to use one type of motor— that is, a type of motor made by one manufacturer. Sizes and adjustments are adapted to fit the special needs of different tractors. The same tendency will be followed in the cases of carburetors, magnetos, radiators, gears, transmissions, differentials, and so on. The development of the auto-

tractors. And the success of the automobile, especially the Ford, clearly demonstrated that farming could be mechanized, too. There were lots of tractors on the market to choose from, and it's clear that the farmer was pretty confused.

A long series of articles by Barton W. Currie in *The Country Gentleman* from April 1916, from one of which this is excerpted, discusses the tractor buyer's dilemma:

Going it blindfolded! That is the situation with the majority of farmers who are picking tractors today. It is not the fault of the

RIGHT
Much of America's most productive farm land has been covered by suburban sprawl. Here is actual proof that Stanford University in California, affectionately known as "The Farm," was really a working farm when this picture was taken in 1940. The stables of late millionaire Leland Stanford now share the campus with a nuclear accelerator, an interesting social comment on the current trends in agriculture and technology. The gigantic native oak trees still exist on "The Farm," living landmarks surviving from rancho to farm to suburb.

Raw horsepower, this hefty hitch is probably rated at a mere two horsepower but it was all that was needed to take care of most of the chores on farms a century ago. Farm technology has come a long way since this early All-Terrain-Vehicle.

The threshing crew has stopped to eat, and the ladies have brought refreshments out to them in the field. This is probably just a stop for lemonade, since the crews generally required mounds of food and the farm wives spent days preparing. Feeding a crew was a major chore that most farm wives dreaded. *Halbe Collection, The Kansas State Historical Society*

LEFT
Mattie Lucas may be a Nebraska pioneer, but she rides like a proper lady, in 1886, with her beautiful embroidered riding gauntlets and her sidesaddle. *Solomon D. Butcher Collection, Nebraska State Historical Society*

mobile has not only made this possible but has really forced it upon the tractor industry as the only economic method of cutting the cost of production.

As a general thing the farmers in this country have been learning a good deal more about the four-cylinder high-speed type of motor in the past few years than they have about one- and two-cylinder oil-burning tractor motors. Manufacturers who

When the Hungry Harvest Hands have gone

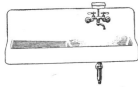

There is room in this Clinton sink for all the dishes from a big dinner. You can have it in three lengths to fit your space: 60½, 74½, 78½ inches. The drainboards are a joy —they are so wonderfully ample, varying from 19¼ to 25¼ inches each in length. And you will find that the "Standard" Swinging Spout Faucet makes dishwashing easier and quicker than ever before.

This Bedford sink is just the thing for a corner or for limited space. You may select it with drainboard either to the right or left and in three lengths: 42½, 52½, and 60½ inches.

This Hudson sink has all the convenience of the most expensive sinks at a more moderate price. The sink with both drainboards is 60 inches long and 22 inches wide. The sink itself is 22 x 22 inches and the drainboards are each 19 inches long.

What a sweep they make of the kitchen's bounties! But what stacks of dishes and pans they leave behind—for you to put a-right.

What a relief to turn to a "Standard" One-piece Sink!

How much the ample drainboards hold —and yet how the stacks of dishes melt away with efficient handling under the Swinging Spout and the Spray. Through, before you know it, and your back saved a mighty burden because the working surface is just right.

Kitchen planners say your sink should save time — energy — footsteps. Does yours stand that test? Only if it gives you all of these:

1. Right height—"yard stick high" is the comfort line.
2. Drainboard and working space a-plenty.
3. One-piece whiteness for health and labor-saving.
4. Faucet-spout that swings where needed.
5. "Tempered" water, or hot or cold, from one spout.
6. Easy cleaning without a joint to hide dirt.
7. Ample width for dishes and pans.
8. Constant drainage—no water standing.
9. Splash-up back to prevent soiling of the wall.

"Standard" Sinks are made that way to lighten women's work.

Standard Sanitary Mfg. Co.
PITTSBURGH

"Standard" PLUMBING FIXTURES

You will find in this "Home Book" just the sink to meet your needs. It will make your kitchen more convenient than you ever dreamed possible and save you hundreds of steps every day. Send today for your copy of the "Home Book" and learn how "Standard" Plumbing Fixtures can be adapted to your home at a surprisingly low cost.

The Country Gentleman, 1926.

Dipping Cattle
Garden City, Ks.

jumped into the tractor game over-night felt that they could supply the popular demand by simply grabbing a four-cylinder automobile motor, common types of automobile carburetors and magnetos and slapping them into any old sort of tractor frame. They suffered from the delusion that if a tractor ran and developed a definite amount of power, that was all that was necessary. They didn't even bother to hitch on a plow and see if the thing would buck or not.

An early gas pump located adjacent to the blacksmith shop on this farm demonstrates the self-sufficiency of this farm operation. When horses began to be replaced by horsepower, many farmers installed their own fuel tanks and pumps. Most farms were too remote to drive to town for a tractor fill-up so maintaining an adequate fuel supply was a smart plan.

Driving the Tractor

Since my grandparents would not keep a horse for our amusement, no matter how much we whined, we had only an occasional tractor ride for amusement. Even then we were not allowed on the tractor itself, just on the hay wagon. Tractors were extremely dangerous, we were all warned, and we were forbidden to play around them. I cannot remember any tractors in my neighborhood that had rollover protection, and the one neighbor who had put an umbrella on his tractor to keep the sun out of his eyes took a lot of ribbing for "getting fancy."

Our tractor rides were limited to sitting on the hay wagon, a very low, wide wagon used to pick up hay bales from the field. If someone was going down to the field to pick up bales and bring them up to the barn, it usually meant a ride. But my grandmother could recall too many broken arms and split lips to allow us to ride without special supervision.

The locusts are out in swarms, eating everything in their path. An infestation could wipe out farms for hundreds of miles. *Wolf Collection, The Kansas State Historical Society*

Crop Dusting

Crop dusters are the fighter pilots in the war against agricultural pests. One duster can save a crop in just a matter of minutes, using an application of spray or dust. This article, which appeared in the *Farm Journal* of December 1939, just before World War II, indicates a permanent role for aeronautics in agriculture.

Airplanes continue to advance in pest fighting. At 100 miles per hour, they do a quicker (and sometimes cheaper) job of spraying or dusting than ground machines. Crack-ups have been reduced greatly, thanks to better-designed planes, more-experienced operators.

Air dusting is still more popular than air spraying. Hoppers are constructed to

Any Farmer Can <u>Now</u> Do His Own Blasting

Atlas Farm Powder never explodes spontaneously or fails to do its work. You can use it without trouble or risk by following instructions that even children understand. Sylvia Richmond, 14-year-old champion tomato grower of Hamilton County, S. C., won because she blasted the subsoil. By using

Atlas Farm Powder
THE SAFEST EXPLOSIVE
The Original Farm Powder

you can improve your soil, get out stumps and shatter boulders quickly and cheaply, blast holes for tree planting, and do many other kinds of farm work in the most economical, up-to-date way. You need no expensive equipment.

Atlas Farm Powder is put up in half-pound charges, ready to use as soon as you attach cap and fuse. It costs little and is sold by dealers near you, who can supply you quickly. We will tell you exactly what you need for any kind of job.

Send Coupon for "Better Farming" Book—FREE

Our large illustrated book, "Better Farming," tells you how to increase fertility of the soil, dig ditches most cheaply, and improve the farm in many ways by using The Safest Explosive. It is valuable to every land owner. Free for the coupon—fill out and mail it now.

ATLAS POWDER COMPANY, General Offices WILMINGTON, DEL.

Birmingham, Boston, Houghton, Joplin, Knoxville, New Orleans, New York, Philadelphia, St. Louis

The threshing crew is in the field although only about half of the manpower needed is posing for the photographer. It usually took two men just to run the steam tractor. It looks like this machine is towing its own fuel wagon. *Halbe Collection, The Kansas State Historical Society*

It looks like this farmer has just acquired a new push mower, a reaper that the horses push rather than pull behind the team. The driver sits where our farmer is standing, and the high seat gives him a good view of his crop, his mower-binder, and his team. *Halbe Collection, The Kansas State Historical Society*

shoot dust earthward at a speed of over 250 miles per hour, which means good coverage. One large western operator charges from 3 to 3-1/2 cents per pound to apply dusts; uses from 10 to 50 pounds per acre. For spraying, he charges 25 to 30 cents an hour.

The Country Gentleman, 1916.

The Country Gentleman, 1916.

CHAPTER SIX

The Farm in the Rural Community

The Country Store

Once the social center for the farm community, the general store or community store was sometimes a combination feed store, grocery store, trading post, post office, filling station, and town hall. In a small town it held onto most of its functions, but as the farmer became less isolated the country store had more competition.

There were several country stores that I had the pleasure to experience. One of the oldest was in Bean Lake, Missouri, and by the time I had the opportunity to patronize the store, its owner, Mrs. Blackmore, was in her 70s. It was old and dusty, with wooden floors, grimy windows, and fading cardboard advertising cards thumb-tacked to the walls, but it was a safe and satisfying destination for two children who wanted to put a dime in the soda machine for a Vess grape pop.

Southern Feed and Seed Store in the French Quarter, New Orleans, Louisiana, 1935. *Walker Evans photo, Library of Congress, FSA*

Small town or big town, when most of the American population lived on farms, they depended on local feed stores for their supplies. Feed stores provided not only feed, seed, and fertilizer, they also sold household goods and hardware. The Fite Feed Store in New Orleans, Louisiana, as it appeared during the Great Depression. *Library of Congress*

Another country store I knew was near Pleasant Hill, Missouri, along the Highway 71 bypass, a store that was closed to the general public. Situated right next to the road, it could have been a profitable business. But the folks who owned the store, and the farm behind it, decided that keeping the store and gas station open seven days a week was too much trouble.

"Too many strangers," they explained. So if they had fresh eggs or fresh zucchini or other local produce, a chalked message would appear on the blackboard out front. And the passing neighbors knew to call before dropping by to pick up their produce.

The largest country store I encountered was near Wheatland, Missouri, but it was not a place for

Seed Store Interior. Note the large selection of canary cages and racks of canary seed. Canaries were a very popular pet on the farm, as well as in towns and cities as this selection of cages indicates. Vicksburg, Mississippi, March 1936. *Walker Evans photo, Library of Congress, FSA*

children to linger. Located near a crossroads, it was a combination store, tavern, and bait shop. The tavern and the store were all part of the same room, and there were always a few old fellows sitting on bar stools, smoking and gabbing with the man at the cash register. Since the Greyhound bus stopped here, there was always a few strangers hanging around, waiting for a ride. As I remember, we were not even allowed to go inside the store but waited outside on the bus bench for Grandpa to bring our candy bars.

A small town at the turn of the century has old false-front buildings and newer brick buildings side by side. The fading letters on the false front say "Studebaker," once one of the finest wagon builders in America (and later a car manufacturer). The establishment next door is probably a general store. Note the bicycles being offered for sale right next to the lawnmowers and other yard implements. *Ritzville Public Library*

Two major rural improvements put country stores out of business: parcel post and improved roads. When farmers could shop by catalog and depend on the post office to deliver goods to their door, it became unnecessary to depend on the selection and prices of the local shopkeeper.

Rural Free Delivery

Is there a mailbox on the road? Then you are in the country where the postal carrier still drives the back roads. Rural Free Delivery (RFD) with its postal delivery boxes on the end of the road, was finally available to farmers around 1904. Although Congress first established a postal service under the federal constitution in 1787, postage stamps and post offices did not come into widespread use until the Civil War. Congress finally got around to providing money to pay mail carriers, but a town had to have a population of at least 10,000 to be eligible for this service. Historian Daniel Boorstin points out that as late as 1890 only about one-fourth of the population had its mail delivered free to its doors. For the majority of Americans—and the majority were on farms—mail had to be picked up at the local post office on the next trip to town.

For many farmers, the weekly trip to the post office was part of the regular round of Saturday chores. In smaller communities the post office was located in the general store and the postmaster was the store proprietor. Naturally, this arrangement provided the store with a steady stream of customers,

You want it, we got it, no problem. Now if we can just remember where we saw it last. . . The local feed and hardware store carried supplies to keep farmers self-sufficient, including, in this case, bicycles (upper right). *Halbe Collection, The Kansas State Historical Society*

coming in to pick up the mail and staying to do a little shopping. It also provided the postmaster (store proprietor) with a paycheck.

But many farmers, especially those who were active members of the Grange movement, had been lobbying hard for postal reforms, and requests for Rural Free Delivery were supported by dozens of local petitions to Congress. There were several factors

behind the push for RFD. One was the farmer's growing resentment of the railroads, a resentment that began to surface soon after the Civil War and helped shape the Grange movement.

A second factor was the relationship between the farm and the town. Shopkeepers preferred having the farmer come to town; it ensured a steady stream of customers. And those businesses that delivered

The country store is, unfortunately, a vanishing tradition in rural areas. The typical store, like this one in Ohio, is a combination post office, gas station, and feed store.

packages and freight via railroad, Wells Fargo and American Express and all the others, also had an interest in maintaining the status quo. But farmers felt they were entitled to the same services as city folk. The debate was long and bitter, as you can tell from the following editorial comments in a 1912 issue of *Farm and Fireside* magazine. The House of Representatives in Washington had delayed passage of RFD legislation, and the magazine editors were furious.

Readers of our fine article on the "home hamper" on page five of this issue will not fail to think of the coming day when the hamper will go from farm to consumer by parcels post, instead of by express. And we hope they will not then fail to turn to the Farmer's Lobby (our column) and read of the contemptible parliamentary trick by which parcels post was beaten by the House.

The entire community of Dorrance, Kansas, in Russell County, centered around the Post Office and the Drug Store. Early midwestern towns had just a few buildings, usually a railroad station and a grain elevator, post office, general store, and blacksmith shop. In the days before Rural Free Delivery (RFD), families in the farm community had to drive to the post office to pick up any mail. In a really small town, the post office might be located inside the drug store or general store. *Halbe Collection, The Kansas State Historical Society*

We have suggested in the past that if farmers choose to consider as enemies those members of Congress who oppose this reform, and to make common cause against them at the polls, no one can say that the farmers are wrong. And the same applies to the Speaker of the House, as he shall be nominated for President. No "hound" has been kicked around more than parcels post . . .

After some spirited debate, the Postmaster General set a standard design around the turn of the century for rural post boxes, replacing the lard buckets, milk pails, and other inventive receptacles that local farmers were providing for mail storage. Daniel Boorstin calls the advent of RFD the most important and most overlooked communications revolution in American history. He notes that RFD "citified the country" and ended the farmer's isolation.

The beginning of RFD was not only the end of isolation, it was a beginning for all sorts of new businesses. Farmers had been reluctant to subscribe to newspapers and periodicals that were outdated and useless by the time they picked up their mail. And mail-order houses such as Montgomery Ward and Sears Roebuck had to depend on slow and expensive railroad delivery for parcels. Now the RFD system and its newer companion, the parcel-post system, ended the isolation and opened an enormous new market to rural America. Hundreds of new businesses opened, served by the mails.

When Will You Get Electricity?

If getting rural mail delivery was a fight that took farmers nearly 40 years to win, getting rural electrical service was nearly as tough. Municipal electrical power was available in major metropolitan areas just after the turn of the century. But most rural areas had to wait until after World War II to get electrical power. Although President Roosevelt had signed the Rural Electrification Act as one of the Depression-era programs, many farms were still using kerosene for light and power until after World War II.

But even after power was available on the farm not everyone used it. Two of our elderly neighbors hooked up just so they could listen to their radios. Ice and wind took the lines down and a rural route with fewer than a dozen customers did not rate a very high service priority. So we did not rely on electric power and always kept an alternate source of heat and light. Our electric stove was backed up by one that ran on LPG. Wood stoves provided another back-up system, and everybody kept kerosene

The canned goods at Scheetz's mercantile store are stacked in attractive pyramids to attract customers. It would seem food display marketing has changed little in the last 80 years. There is some penny candy in the front case and a crate of fresh cabbages right next to the clerk. *Halbe Collection, The Kansas State Historical Society*

Market day with a livestock auction is held once a week in Kidiron, Ohio. Amish farmers line up to buy and sell all sorts of farm produce as well as livestock. Local markets like this are held nearly every day of the week in one little town or another in the Amish communities. This type of market can still commonly be found in Pennsylvania, Ohio, Indiana, Illinois, Missouri, and other places with Amish communities.

lamps for light. Candles were forbidden; the risk of fire was too great.

If you grew up in town, you might think that farmers were just impoverished backward folk who were reluctant to electrify their farms because they were too cheap, too stubborn, or too ignorant.

Nothing could be further from the truth. Though farmers were very reluctant to electrify their operations, it was usually for less obvious reasons.

In the first place farmers did not need electrical power. Many farms already had a little gasoline generator or similar power plant, all the power the farmer

Steam traction engines were used in rural areas to build roads. J.I. Case built big steamers like this one until 1924, and there were still lots of them in service until World War II. The picture is identified as M.L. Neil's road building outfit in Rock County, Wisconsin. Neil has about a dozen haul wagons lined up behind his steamer. *Ritzville Public Library*

Rural Free Delivery was the second step linking farmers to the markets in town. The railroad provided the first step. *Halbe Collection, The Kansas State Historical Society*

To the often-isolated farmer and his family, Rural Free Delivery was a vital link to the rest of the country. *The Country Gentleman*, 1916.

available to everyone who wanted it. This excerpt by Charles Moreau Harger from an article in *The Country Gentleman* in 1918 is a good example of the propagada efforts. It's important to remember that articles like this were actually aimed more at the farm wife than her husband.

When we spent the evening with the Graftons 12 miles from town, we were observant of the modern touch in the comfortable sitting room. Electric lights, a whirring fan and even tea served by the hostess from a little electrically heated kettle made it a little less like the usual picture of a farm home.

Stepping from the door at departure, we peered blinkingly into the dark, trying to locate the motor car. "Wait a minute," ordered the host. He hurried to the end of the porch and turned a

felt he needed. In the second place, rural electrification was not that reliable; bad weather could leave a farm stranded. And finally, farmers were very independent. Many of them remembered when the railroad came to town and promised to be the farmer's friend. Grange members and farm co-ops were still fighting tariff battles with the railroads, so farmers were naturally skeptical about any large outside organization.

But farm magazines promoted electrification for years, and gradually service became

The farm wife's most important crop was children, and many folks felt that you could only raise happy, healthy children in a rural atmosphere. Bareheaded, bare-legged, and bareback, these little Kansas girls are enjoying their pony. *The Kansas State Historical Society*

The Oak Grove School, a one-room school, is still in use in Jamesport, Missouri, for the Amish schoolchildren. This is a relatively new structure, built to accommodate all grades. Children usually attend classes until the age of 14. The horse is waiting to take children home after class.

button set in the wall. Suddenly the entire farmyard and the driveway were flooded with light. On top of the windmill tower blazed a hundred-power electric lamp, furnishing an illumination like a section of the Midway Plaisance. Standing alone in the night, its brilliancy was doubtless exaggerated, but the result was decidedly effective.

"Take a look at our stock before you go," eagerly urged our entertainer. One, two, half a dozen lights twinkled in a line along a cement walk that led to the barns. Entering the horse barn, the owner turned another button and the interior was as light as day. Up in the haymow [shone] a lamp; along the stables was another line, and over the grain bins gleamed yet others.

continued on page 126

Land Grant Colleges and Agricultural Extension

We owe many debts to our farming forefathers that we can never repay. One item that usually gets omitted altogether from the balance sheet is the establishment of land-grant colleges and experiment stations. The Morrill Act of 1862 provided for the establishment of agricultural colleges in each state. Some schools, such as Purdue University in Indiana, were separate agricultural colleges, while others in Wisconsin and Illinois were organized as colleges within their respective state universities.

Arguments for a system of agricultural colleges had been circulated for many years before the law was finally passed. But members of Congress, many of whom were practicing farmers at the time, realized that education, especially education about agricultural production and technology, was essential. Tuition would be free. And it was this first group of college-trained farmers and children of farmers who provided the nucleus of faculty and staff in the field stations. Many land-grant colleges, the University of Wisconsin, Kansas State University, and more than a dozen others, were turning out students long before 1900. These graduates would constitute the first great tide of technical talent that lifted agriculture to new production levels.

American agricultural abundance is based upon a systematic approach to agriculture. Ag schools and their experiment stations worked hand in hand to determine which crops and livestock were best suited to local soils and climate. Realizing that many farmers could not take the time or afford the enormous risks to experiment, ag school farms developed the most promising innovations for local farmers. The Hatch Act was passed in 1887 to establish agricultural experiment stations under the supervision of the colleges in each state.

The third element of the agricultural-education system showed up just before World War I. The universities and the farm experiment stations were joined by a system of county agents and demonstrators who took the improvements from the laboratory to the farmer in the field. The agricultural extension service really got going around 1914, just before World War I. County agents, home-demonstration agents, and soil-conservation agents all began to work with farmers and students to teach the value of better farming techniques.

I would be misleading you if I let you think that all of these developments took place in a smooth and orderly manner. Many farmers resented the idea of a farm agent or demonstrator—some book-learned pipsqueak—telling them what to do. And the farmers resented paying for the lesson even more. This article from the editorial page of *The New England Homestead*, January 4, 1913, lets the bureaucrats know just how farmers felt about the new proposal for a county agent.

Is the farmer being oversubsidized? Is too much being done FOR him and too little done BY him? These questions are being raised by a number of our farmers, who are solicited to take part in the many "uplift" efforts now being made.

In each state the board of agriculture or similar state body, the agricultural college and experiment station and the various farm organizations are all trying in various ways to promote agriculture. Now comes the United States Department of Agriculture with a proposition to supply to each county, a demonstrator in efficient farming, providing the banking or other interests in the county will pay half the salary and expenses of such a man.

In some cases these federal demonstrators assume to know it all, they fail to co-operate with the agencies already established in the state, and convey the impression that the federal bureau is the "only means of grace" for the farmer! That sort of dictation is frequently resented by the farmers, as well as by the colleges, stations and other state institutions.

"Fears have been expressed that college men may not like practical farming"

Farm and Fireside, 1912.

But the county agents and demonstrators prevailed, and since many of them were the freshly trained offspring of proud local farmers, products of the local agriculture colleges, their progressive ideas eventually won over more-conservative opinion. The vitality and enthusiasm of the agents, combined with demonstrated financial benefit to the local farmer, changed local attitudes.

Agricultural engineering students evaluate an assortment of farm machinery during a college class. Students dressed in suits and ties and usually hats, a notable difference from today's budding scholars. *The Kansas State Historical Society*

Experiment stations growing test crops assisted local farmers. This station specialized in growing pasture and forage crops. *Wolf Collection, The Kansas State Historical Society*

Little one-room schools became "consolidated" but educational support still came from the local community. This country school in Kansas is being painted by local people in preparation for a new school term. It's a new building which houses several grades, students traveling by horse or by gas-powered buggy to attend school. Students usually attended school until eighth grade, about age 14 or so. High school attendance was less common, partly because older children were needed to help on the farm and partly due to lack of high schools in rural communities. Good roads and the auto industry helped improve the ability to acquire an education. *Halbe Collection, The Kansas State Historical Society*

Continued from page 122

The hog sheds, the cattle sheds, the garage, the barnyard with a powerful light swung high in its center, making every corner bright—the same story over and over. I thought of the old fire-setting lantern I had carried while doing the chores on the boyhood farm back in western New York. It was some change.

The Volunteer Fire Brigade

An important institution in many small town and farm communities was the volunteer fire department. While most fire brigades had an important safety responsibility, many became more of a social organization. The community would gather to hold dinners, raffles, and other fund-raising events to get enough money to buy a pumping

Baker's School No.12, an abandoned community school in southeastern Nebraska. These one-room schools began to disappear around 1920, when improved roads, gasoline-powered school buses, and consolidated school districts offered students educational advantages that were not available in the one-room school.

rig. Then they would find a garage or shed with a central location to store their new truck.

Usually the fire shed had a tower with a whistle. If there was a fire in the neighborhood the alarm whistle would sound, followed by shorter toots that would signal the approximate location. Volunteers could then park their plows and head their pickups to the reported location.

The local fire whistle was used as a warning whistle for other potential disasters such as

impending tornadoes or rising flood waters and during community-defense drills.

The Community School

The one-room school, frequently called a country school or district school, was a local institution shared by farm families within an area of several miles. It was usually a community project, built and supported by local farmers out of farm profits. They were built to be within walking distance of

The one-room schoolhouse was an American institution from coast to coast. This one is in Copperopolis, California. The steeple held a bell and the flagpole.

RIGHT
With 11 girls and 18 boys in this class portrait, it's no wonder the teacher looks a bit frazzled. The picture is unidentified but was probably taken in eastern Washington around the turn of the century. *Collection of the Ritzville Public Library*

children. Schoolteachers were hired by a small committee of local farmers who contributed either money or other goods to provide their room and board.

One of the best descriptions of life in a country school appears in the wonderful series of books, *Little House on the Prairie*, written by Laura Ingalls Wilder. She vividly describes her experiences, first as a student and then as a teacher, trying to manage her pupils in a little one-room school on the frontier. One-room schools began to be replaced by consolidated school districts about 1920, but progress was slowed by the Depression and World War II. I attended a suburban consolidated school district for a while after World War II, and the ride to class on a snowy morning was much more exciting than any lesson the teacher could prepare. Buses frequently slid off the narrow back roads and had to wait for a truck to pull them from the ditch. Since many of the bus drivers were also schoolteachers, classes would be suspended for several hours until the teacher finally arrived.

Abandoned farmhouse, part of the cycle of decay and growth on the farm. Less than 2 percent of the American population is now actively engaged in farming, and abandoned farmsteads are a common sight. Although the house itself may be abandoned, the fields may still be tilled by neighboring farmers. Improvements in mechanization mean that a single farmer can now efficiently manage hundreds of acres.

The first school built in Union Township in Santa Clara County, California, was built on skids so that the little schoolhouse could be relocated every year or so. This allowed such costs as providing a site, water, and fuel for the stove to be shared until a permanent site could be found.

Typical school attendance was limited to children between the ages of six or seven and about age thirteen. While an eighth-grade education was fairly common, what we now know as a high-school education was not considered necessary for success in farming. In addition, it was felt that young people who spent time in a high school some distance from home were especially vulnerable to bad moral influences. Attending school was a luxury, because frequently a child could not be spared from the regular responsibilities of farm chores.

Consolidating the rural schools—that is, combining the ungraded one-room school into a larger building with grades based on age and ability—reportedly originated in Massachusetts as early as 1869. But an overwhelming move toward consolidated schools did not start until the first two decades of this century.

Movies on the Farm

The United States Department of Agriculture has always been extremely progressive and pioneered the use of the "educational film," using movies to train farmers and influence agricultural programs. An article from the *Farm Journal* in 1924 demonstrates how sophisticated the USDA had become:

"Book farming" may have 16,000,000 advocates and as many traducers, but it has been displaced in a good many places by something new. The new something is "film farming." Already there are thousands, tens of thousands of farmers, who, through watching a motion picture, have learned some new kink, got some new light on better ways to make the old farm pay, of

The local telephone operator. This friendly lady is identified as "Bernice at the Home Telephone Office." She is wearing a headset, and the long cord from the earpiece plugs into her switchboard allowing her to answer calls and personally connect her customers' phones to one another.

The Theilan elevator was owned by a local farm family near Dorrance, Kansas. It's a good example of a local farmer branching out into related businesses when there was additional capital to invest. *Halbe Collection, The Kansas State Historical Society*

making the old farm more comfortable for mother and the kids, of repelling the foes and fungi that puncture the pocketbook. That is certain. The United States Department of Agriculture had signed and documentary proof of it in letters from users of better-farming films.

Farmers were not the only audience for the USDA films. Since the films were free to schools or available at a very small cost, they were the movies that we saw most often in the classroom when I was growing up.

The local telephone operator usually had the switchboard in the living room of her home in order to handle emergency calls day or night. The charming picture on the calendar (1910) behind the visitor echoes the scene in the room. *Halbe Collection, The Kansas State Historical Society*

One County Agent did all these things in the course of a year. *The Country Gentlemen,* 1916.

CHAPTER SEVEN
Social Life

*V*eterans' Groups: Maintaining the Union

The opening of the West took place at the same time the Civil War was underway. President Lincoln signed the Homestead Act during the second year of the Civil War, so the wartime events were still fresh in the minds of many of the American families who moved west. For many homesteading pioneers, the choice of moving to a new community was determined by whether the residents favored the Union or the Confederacy during the Great Conflict. The Union Township in Santa Clara Valley, California, is a reminder that these early settlers had favored the North in the Great Conflict and Southern sympathizers were not welcome.

Across rural America, visiting the local cemetery on Memorial Day was an annual event, and my grandmother was visibly annoyed when we misbehaved. By the time we were adolescents we refused to accompany her to the parade and picnic, whining that it

It wasn't much of a town—just a hotel, a post office, and a drug store—but the folks in Dorrance, Kansas, still had a motoring club. Farmers have always been interested in new technology and this motoring club should remind us that not only were farmers pioneering new land, they were interested in trying new innovations as well. It's also a reminder that many farmers prospered and could afford to buy autos and motorcycles for "touring." Remember that horses had some limitations—if nothing else, they smelled like, well, horses. And their acceleration and range were pretty limited when compared to an early Harley or Indian. So which would you choose?
Halbe Collection, The Kansas State Historical Society

Maintaining the Union, the surviving members of the Grand Army of the Republic celebrates July 4 with a parade and picnic. Hot weather in West Union, Nebraska, has forced these participants and their families to remove their coats and uniforms. This patriotic celebration was held in 1912, nearly half a century after the Civil War ended. *Solomon D. Butcher Collection, Nebraska State Historical Society*

was s-o-o-o-o boring! Grandma's family had fought in the Great War and every May we heard stories about Obed Beardslee—"deaf as a post"—an artilleryman for the Union. He lost his hearing from firing the cannon. A large man for the time, over six feet tall and weighing 200 pounds, he carried the flag in the annual Memorial Day parade in Lowry City, Missouri.

Photographs taken before 1900, appearing in dozens of old family albums, usually show an Independence Day parade or picnic. Frequently, there is a long line of grizzled old men, wearing parts of their old military uniforms and carrying the flags and banners from their local volunteer regiments. They were usually the remnants of the local regiment of the Grand Army of the Republic, known as the G.A.R. Like today's Veterans of Foreign Wars—the

VFW groups that represent the thousands of military veterans from World Wars I and II, the Korean Conflict, and Vietnam—the survivors of the Civil War were the honored guests at patriotic celebrations.

Today, many of the old soldiers have faded away and most of their civic activities are forgotten, but for nearly a century after its conclusion, the Civil War continued to affect small-town life. Social circles and business relationships were determined by your family's participation in the war. "Yankee" or "Rebel" were either accolade or epithet well into the 20th century.

The Ice-Cream Social

My grandfather always referred to this as "the sociable," and he refused to go. Looking back, it

It looks like a Sunday school class with all of the children in their best clothes. There are half a dozen shiny apples proudly displayed, perhaps awarded as prizes for outstanding recitation. *Ritzville Public Library*

seems to me that the ice-cream socials were attended mostly by women, children, and young single people. Maybe Gramps did not want to put on a dress shirt to go sit and eat ice cream. Since my grandmother always made a few extra goodies when she was baking for the social, he could eat his cake in solitary bliss.

Ice cream was a rare treat, since refrigerators were still not in widespread use. While there were two farm wives on our road who owned a "deep-freeze," a large new freezer that kept food at zero degrees, the freezers were typically used for meat and vegetables; there was no room for anything as frivolous as ice cream. And the tiny little freezer in our home refrigerator could barely hold ice cubes. So ice cream, especially handmade ice cream, took some effort and was always a treat.

Ice-cream socials were summertime fund-raising events, organized by the Methodists or the Baptists, and usually held in the church hall. Since the Catholics were allowed to drink, dance, and play cards, their fund-raising efforts focused on bingo nights and polka parties. That left the remaining churches with the more sedate fund-raising activities. But religious affiliation was neither a bar nor a requirement to attend a "sociable," and the entire community was invited.

Cultural Improvement and the Chatauqua

Life in a rural community could be bleak without cultural and social amenities. Farm wives were determined to have the same social advantages as their city sisters, and many belonged to several groups that promoted intellectual and social improvement.

Some women organized local libraries; others formed singing societies and musical groups. While the local churches usually coordinated Bible study groups or local aid societies to help the poor and ailing, it was the rural social organizations that brought amusement to farm life.

In the days before radio, and even after radio was available, traveling tent shows provided occasional amusement. The grandest show of rural entertainment available was the Chatauqua, an extravaganza of educational lectures, presented over several days at a campground or resort. Named after the rural New York resort where they originated, the shows became so popular that they traveled from town to town and were presented throughout the Midwest during the summers.

The Chatauqua presented famous speakers, or actors and actresses, in programs that had an effect on local opinion for months after the tents had folded. Families would pack up their own tents and travel to the towns where the program was underway. It was an opportunity for several days of socializing, relaxation, and entertainment.

The tradition persisted until around World War II. Today it is probably best remembered as the training ground for dozens of young stars. Various entertainers who went on to wider fame in television

The Country Gentleman, 1926.

and the movies started their careers in vaudeville, in summer stock, or on the Chatauqua circuit.

State Fairs

The agricultural fair, the state fair, and county fair as we know them today, had their origin in the old-world market days and fairs. The early European fairs were primarily markets where produce and livestock were bought and sold. But gradually there evolved contests in which cattle and horses were compared and judged, probably to demonstrate desirable breeding characteristics.

State and county fairs have provided a farmer's entertainment for hundreds of years. Sponsored by the agricultural societies in conjunction with the local state or county government, the fairs are a unique marketplace. They are where many farmers go to quietly check on the performance of new equipment, new breeding methods, and the comparative success of their neighbors.

Farm shows and agricultural societies have flourished and faded, coming back to life and changing the focus of their programs as local farmers have changed. It may be a surprise to find that today's fairs are not greatly different from those of times past. Car races and tractor pulls have been part of the show since these machines first showed up on the

Chautauquas, or tent meetings, were important social, cultural, and educational events in rural areas. Originating in New York State, a Chautauqua was a week-long tent meeting offering plays, lectures, poetry reading, and a chance to meet folks from other parts of the world. *The Kansas State Historical Society*

farm. Salesmen and demonstrators have always used these fairs to showcase their products. And local community groups have always used the state fair to promote their activities. Everyone from Dad all the way to Junior's pet white mice can come home with an award ribbon; there is a contest for everybody.

A fair is the best place to sample local food. Peach pie or strawberry shortcake, strudels, doughnuts, and cobblers—local produce prepared by local cooks. There are some snacks that are a traditional part of fairs and carnivals, like cotton candy or funnel cakes or those deep-fried corn dogs. You can find them at other community events like ball games, but we all know they taste best at the fair.

Fremont's Big Show

County fairs, state fairs, and local competitions were annual events for many farm families, who planned a major excursion once a year to exhibit prize-winning livestock or produce. But farmers were

A dozen young people gather on the front porch, and we can only speculate about the event. Is it a birthday party, a singing group, or just a social? *Ritzville Public Library*

interested in other events, and the National Farm Tractor Demonstration held in Fremont, Nebraska, in 1916 drew an amazing 50,000 spectators. The show was a debut for the first Ford tractor, and Henry Ford himself was in attendance to hear comments.

This historic show marked a significant milestone, one that was recognized by many of the spectators and participants. There was an awareness of the coming mechanization of agriculture, a future that would soon be a reality. The significance was underlined by the amazing fact that 50,000 farmers would drive county roads to converge on Fremont. For those of us who now read historic accounts of the traffic jams created by the event, it seems incredible that there were so many motor cars in rural areas.

As one reporter wrote,

A statistician of the Fremont Board of Trade figured that, sure enough, Nebraska farmers burned up half-a-million gallons of gasoline getting to the show and home again. The Fremont candy kitchen made a million sandwiches or thereabouts. A Fremont traffic constable developed paralysis of the right arm directing traffic. Between four and five thousand visiting automobiles streamed through Main Street and thence on out Lincoln Highway to the tractor grounds on the biggest day of the show. The cars were parked along a mile and a half of roadway, from five to fifty deep. It was on Wednesday, August ninth, that the local papers counted 50,000 folks as holiday visitors to their trim little city and its prairie suburbs. Fifty thousand "tractor fans" may be an overcount of a few battalions, but as there were no turnstiles to check up by, why not give the local optimists all the benefit of the doubt.

As the reporter concluded, Fremont "was a watershed event; one of the most important moments in American agricultural history."

The Grange

A few communities still have their Grange Hall, but Grange meetings have nearly disappeared from the calendars of farm life. During the 100 or so years that the Grange was in existence, it was probably the most important political force on the farm frontier. The Federal Farm Loan program, agricultural price supports, and uniform freight tariffs for farm products were just some of the many agricultural programs initiated by the Grange. The Grange lobbied for Blue Cross medical insurance and promoted the Montgomery Ward catalog sales company. It's hard to imagine what America would be like without the Grange.

Founded in 1869 just after the Civil War, the Grange was one of the strongest and most important political voices in America until after World War II. Sometimes known as the National Grange of the Patrons of Husbandry, the Grange was a fraternal organization or club, and its purpose was to unite farmers and give them a collective voice.

The organization sprang from the need to assist farmers with land-grant problems, and once the organization became known, new chapters of it spread like prairie wildfire.

While Grange organizers proclaimed lofty ideals about the future of agriculture, there is no doubt that the backbone of the Grange movement was strongly rooted in members' opposition to the American railroads. Since most railroads were first created with grants of government land, and since many homesteaders were encouraged to buy this railroad land and send produce to market via the local railroad, it was only logical that farmers expected a cooperative attitude. Instead, farmers felt the railroads took unfair advantage of them by setting exorbitant freight rates in a market monopoly. When farmers sought equity in local courts and legislatures, the railroads attempted to buy local judges, representatives, and members of Congress. The Grange took on the railroads and fought the oppressive tariffs.

Small prairie towns were centered around two or three structures: the train station, the water tower, and the grain elevator. Frequently a co-op venture used by all the farmers in the area, the elevator stored all the harvested grain until it could be shipped to market. This grain elevator is combined with a flouring mill in Ritzville, Washington. *Ritzville Public Library*

Mount Ayr cemetery near Cameron, Missouri. Little rural burying grounds like this one are found throughout rural America, still in use by the local community. Tiny churches and their cemeteries are commonly found in the countryside, usually located several miles from the nearest town. Frequently served by a traveling minister, services were often nondenominational. Services were more of a social occasion than a religious rite, neighbors putting aside their religious affiliations to hear the only preacher available. Cemeteries were established away from inhabited areas for sanitation reasons.

The father of the Grange movement was a Boston Yankee turned Minnesota farmer, Oliver Hudson Kelley. Kelley had some experience as a reporter and telegrapher, wrote many articles about farming for farm papers, and became a regular contributor to the Federal Department of Agriculture.

Kelley's agricultural reports won him a clerkship in the Department of Agriculture during the last years of the Civil War, 1864 and 1865. At the end of the war, President Andrew Johnson sent Kelley to make a survey of agricultural conditions in the South. Surveying the devastation, Kelley developed the idea of an association of farmers, North and South, to improve conditions. Since he was a member of the Masonic lodge, he envisioned a fraternal group for farmers similar to the Masonic Order.

The birthday of the Patrons of Husbandry is recognized as December 4, 1867. Supported by six other gentlemen, Kelley went on the road, attempting to organize local chapters of his fraternity. Organizing was difficult, but economic conditions in farming supported the formation of Grange groups.

The Grange developed and supported buying co-ops for farmers, getting good prices for bulk purchases of seed and machinery. The early success of retailer Montgomery Ward & Company was largely due to support by local Grange chapters. Farmers frequently had difficulty buying merchandise on credit. A "Monkey Ward" order, however, guaranteed by a local Grange chapter, ensured delivery of items ordered from Ward's catalog.

It was the Grange that shaped the development of farm education through its support of the establishment of land-grant colleges and the development of agricultural extension. The Grange supported the expansion of the postal service to farms with Rural

Culture and self-improvement were important in rural America. This library was built in 1884, and regular meetings of local literary societies provided an important opportunity to get together. *The Kansas State Historical Society*

Free Delivery. The Grange advocated the establishment of a parcel-post delivery system as early as 1887, although the legislation for a postal system for small packages was not enacted until 1913. The Grange supported the Pure Food and Drug Act, better highways and road systems, and the temperance movement.

Co-ops

Farming co-ops are an interesting institution in American agribusiness. They are an important social and economic force in agriculture, and we can recognize the significance of these groups by the magnitude of their contributions. Since many co-ops are omitted by conventional history books and ignored by business classes, their impact is sometimes overlooked.

There are many types of farming co-ops, and we shall mention only a few. There are the co-ops that were formed by a group of neighbors with

mutual economic needs. Threshing rings are one example. A "ring" is a group of neighbors, relatives, or friends who help each other at harvest time. One individual will usually own a thresher and the others will help pay in some manner, either by contributing labor or part of the crop after harvesting. Threshing rings and co-op grain elevators at the railroad are two of the most common co-op organizations in the wheat belt.

Rural water districts, fire districts, or flood control districts are another type of co-operative organization. In this situation there is usually a need to levy a tax of some sort in order to pay for improvements or hazard protection that would benefit the entire community. Barbecues and dances are big annual fundraising events for volunteer fire departments in many communities.

Another important early co-operative organization was the school district. Organized by local farmers who frequently took turns boarding and housing

The Country Gentleman, 1916.

Two chairs, no waiting. The local post office may have been an important social center but with two barbers, this tonsorial parlor in Western Kansas was also a hub of activity. *Halbe Collection, The Kansas State Historical Society*

the teachers, the rural school boards were one of the earliest and most widespread rural co-operative groups. Since school districts needed to be supported by local taxes, an organization to fund a local school was one of the first formed in most rural communities.

Many co-operative groups were developed around a specific commodity or crop. The Wisconsin Dairy Association was an early association which functioned as both a milk producers processing co-op and an organization that improved breeding stock. The American Hereford Association was also organized by cattle breeders to improve their breed; Charolais, Shorthorns, and Aberdeen Angus all have their respective co-operative associations.

Today, most farmers and growers are members of some association that addresses the needs of their particular products. The California raisin growers have a co-op, so do the wine makers. The pork producers and the dairy associations now have marketing and public relations organizations that not only keep an eye on the marketplace, but lobby for pro-

These handsome fellows and their manager are part of the Dorrance, Kansas, baseball team. Rural communities enjoyed the same sports and amusements as folks living in town. After the establishment of agricultural colleges and consolidated school districts, rural residents became better acquainted with fellow students from neighboring communities. Telephones and the auto encouraged frequent communication. Sports rivalries are a long-standing tradition in the rural Midwest as any diehard Cornhusker or Aggie fan will confirm. *Halbe Collection, The Kansas State Historical Society*

tective legislation when needed. Sunkist was a co-op for citrus growers and was first founded in 1895. It has been looking after the interests of its members for a century.

Like the medieval guildhalls of Europe and protective trade unions in other industries, American farmers developed cooperatives and mar-

RIGHT
Bad weather frequently brought communities together. The utility pole was damaged in an ice storm and was being reinforced as a temporary measure. *Halbe Collection, The Kansas State Historical Society*

Some farmers were well educated and well-to-do, always interested in new technology and new methods to improve productivity. And since farm youngsters learned to drive the family tractor as soon as their feet could reach the pedals, driving an automobile was probably a more common activity on the farm than it was in town after the turn of the century. Out for a spin in the new Reo, members of the Theilen family and their friends stop for their portrait. The motorcycle is an American, manufactured in Chicago from 1911 through 1914. *Halbe Collection, The Kansas State Historical Society*

keting organizations to protect their own economic interests.

Funeral Pie

Rural funerals were important social events, and stories of memorable wakes were sometimes retold with the same enthusiasm used for recalling holiday gatherings. The guest list and menu were recounted as were details of the wake, the sermon, and any other significant or interesting conversations. I can remember my grandmother saying with a laugh, "Mama would have loved her funeral. Everybody she knew was there." The best funerals were family reunions; the worst funerals were when the recently departed was a child or an accident victim.

Alice Bird recalls memories of funerals in the 1930s: "There was seldom a service held at the funeral home. One room of the home of the deceased (usually the parlor) was cleared of all furniture so the casket could be properly placed for viewing. The funeral director hung a black wreath or bow on the door of the home. Friends and family took turns sitting with the body, so there was always someone in attendance. Neighbors and friends brought in food to serve the family and its visitors. Raisin pie has often been called 'funeral pie' because it kept without refrigeration and was easy to transport."

This custom was called a wake, a procedure that has nearly disappeared today. Bird recalls that the wakes of Germans and Irish, who were usually Lutheran or Catholic, tended to be a little rowdy and lighthearted by the time the mourners had consumed whatever spirits were available. But Baptists and Campbellites, she reports, were extremely sober in every respect. Even a smile would be a show of disrespect for the dearly departed.

Courage, modesty, faith, unselfishness, and endurance . . . these Kansas matrons demonstrate all the virtues embroidered on their banners. Lodges and their ladies' auxiliaries were important social institutions at the turn of the century. *Halbe Collection, The Kansas State Historical Society*

The True Life of a Farm Wife

The *Farmer's Handbook* shows a photograph of a farm wife sitting on top of a horse-drawn wagon with the caption, "Woman's sphere may be the home, the nursery, and the kitchen, but many a farm success has come through her aid and influence outside their limits." In smaller print the picture is subtitled, "This sort of family cooperation is not so unusual. But how often do we find the farmer helping with the dishes or the house cleaning?"

It wasn't the hard work or the economic uncertainty that took its toll on the farm wife; it was the isolation. Before telephones, radios, and free mail delivery, the farm wife was frequently alone in the house. Only the wealthy could afford an extra horse and wagon to make social calls. So unless the farm family was willing to take a hike to go visiting, or wait until the farmer finished plowing and the horses were rested, they were alone.

In agricultural Santa Clara County, California, the farm wives of the Union Township took a lesson from their city sisters with their calling cards and "at home" days. In 1892 the farm wives declared Thursday as their visiting day, and on that day they would all converge on the home of one of the members, establishing the oldest Women's Club in the state of California.

In those days the local farm ladies would walk or hitch a ride on the back of a passing wagon to spend the day with their friends, sewing and visiting. This little group in the West Valley started the local school district, the local fire-protection district, and organized hundreds of fund-raising events over the years. The Union School District and the thousands of residents in suburban West Valley now owe their comfortable life to these first farm wives. Around 1910 the ladies built a clubhouse on land donated by one of the original members, and they have shared their clubhouse with their community for over a century.

Rural clubs sometimes called Farmer's Clubs or Women's Clubs were commonplace, some more prosperous than others. News of their activities appears in an occasional article in the farm magazines. *The Country Gentleman* of 1916 features clubs in Dayton, Ohio, and Walworth, Wisconsin. The Walworth Club has just built itself a $10,000 clubhouse with earnings from a series of lecture courses. Not to be outdone, the women in Dayton have raised enough money to drain and repair a mile of bad road.

And in Payne County, Oklahoma, farmers looking for a little recreation built themselves a fishing lake. During the middle of World War II, the local farmer's club was meeting in a local filling station, so they built a facility that could be used by the entire family. Calling themselves the Spit and Whittle Club, they found 20 acres for a country club and built themselves a 6-acre lake for fishing.

Isolation in the Nebraska Sand Hills

While many farm families were isolated, they were not always alone and lonely. This excerpt from a 1918 article in *The Country Gentleman* tells how farm families in Nebraska solved the problem.

"Have you ever traveled miles and miles without seeing a sign of habitation,

Two young ladies opt for a fleet Yale motorbike to escape the drudgery of saddling up a smelly horse to a heavy buggy, just to get a ride to town. The dainty dresses and pretty hats suggest they are just posing. Motorcycling on the rural roads of the early 1900s was far too dirty for such finery. *Halbe Collection, The Kansas State Historical Society*

then suddenly glimpsed a little shack standing out like a sentinel in a vast stretch of prairie land so heavily sanded that vegetation was sparse?" began Mrs. Hudson. "Can you realize what it means for a woman to go with the man she promised to take for better or worse and to make a home in such desolation? Can you imagine what it means to go for as long as a year without seeing another woman?

"I was a school teacher before I married my cowboy husband," said Mrs. Hudson, "and when we made our home in the sand hills six miles from Valentine, I found the isolation almost unbearable. The men had their dehornings and brandings, which satisfied their social cravings. The women had nothing. It was no unusual thing for a woman to live for a year without seeing one of her sex.

"It was a cowboy husband who solved the problem and all but handed us our club in his sombrero. He offered to act as housekeeper and nurse once every three weeks if the other men would do likewise. They have made our club possible for three years now by relieving their wives of the household work for one day out of every 21. There are now 25 women in our club, and we all have to travel from 8 to 20 miles to the club meetings. We tuck our sewing bags under our saddles and ride away from home in the early morning and we are gone all day. We do the work planned by our hostess: card wool, make comforters, piece quilts. We

Dr. Ella S. Webb's magazine for farm women was the first published by a woman, and was also the first to cover important topics such as child development and nutrition. The magazine was so popular and influential that it inspired a network of women's clubs throughout the upper Midwest. The magazine eventually became part of *The Farm Journal*. *The Farmer's Wife*, 1912

have no officers or dues. Anyone who is a neighbor is a member. Community interest is developed, ideas of domestic science are exchanged, the mothers go home with glowing cheeks and sparkling eyes, all ready for the next day's duties."

Farm Women and Insanity

But isolation had its darker side, especially for homesteaders who had little community support. From the same page of *The Country Gentleman* was this accompanying article.

Years ago someone wrote: "No greater indictment of the life led by the average farm woman could be imagined than the records which show that the average farm women, more than others of their sex, are driven insane by the lonely life and hours of drudgery which are their lot."

That statement has spread until it has come to be accepted as an economic axiom. Now it is branded as false by one of the staff workers in the United States Department of Agriculture, who has been working for 20 years to either substantiate the statement or refute it. He can refute it.

"Tracing this statement backward," said the investigator, "[we] found [that it] originated with a woman who was a prolific writer on domestic subjects. A letter of inquiry addressed to her brought no response. A physician who writes popular articles on health and disease gave his endorsement to the assertion in a recent year. He was also requested to supply the facts upon which he rested his conclusion. He had none, but he had an uncertain impression that the superintendent of an insane asylum in the Middle West had given him the idea. A letter to that superintendent brought this letter. 'My personal experience in investigating the causes of insanity, predisposing and exciting, both mental and physical, has always brought me to the conclusion that a farmer's wife is less likely to become insane than the wife of a man who lives in the city.'"

An official of an insane hospital in another state of the Middle West wrote:

From the opening of this hospital until October 1912, we admitted 5,363 foreign-born and but 2,900 native-born men and women. Of the 2,070 women for whom we were able to obtain occupations of husbands or fathers, but 237 had husbands or fathers who were farmers and 318 who were farm laborers." Therefore, said the investigator, "the farms contributed only 27 percent of the insane women, while the farming population of the state is 40 percent of the total."

*A*ppendices
Eyewitness to Farm History—
Magazines and Photographs

Looking at Photographs

There are a number of ways of looking at farm history, and one of the most interesting is to look at the photographs and magazines that were produced at the time. We are extremely fortunate that several state archives have photography collections that feature farm photographs.

The archival photographic resources used for this book include the Halbe Collection and the Wolf Collection in the Kansas State Historical Society Archives in Topeka, as well as the Solomon Butcher Collection from the Nebraska State Historical Archives in Omaha.

In addition, we have used images from the San Jose Historical Museum in San Jose, California, and an interesting but uncatalogued collection of farm photographs from the City Library in Ritzville, Washington. Copies of most of the photographs in this book are available for sale from the historical societies that own them.

Several of the collections are unique because they represent the photographer's carefully considered portrait of contemporary life in his community. Unlike the pictures of studio photographers or untrained snapshot enthusiasts, most of the images presented here represent the work of an individual who carefully considered his subject material before he committed the image to a glass plate.

Solomon Butcher was a homesteader in Custer County, Nebraska, in the late 1880s. A part-time photographer, his goal was to publish a photographic history of Custer County, which he finally accomplished in 1901. The volume was such a success that he planned similar books on nearby Buffalo and Dawson counties, and photographed there, too. But the later books were not produced, and he decided to move to Texas in 1912. He sold his collection of plates to the Nebraska State Historical Society at that time.

Farm and Fireside masthead, 1914.

The Collectible Farm Magazine

Magazine historian Frank Luther Mott reports that there were 139 magazines devoted to general agriculture in the late 1890s. When you include periodicals aimed at a specific group—threshermen, fruit growers, or sheepmen—the number nearly triples. In general, however, the agricultural magazines fall into three major classifications: general-interest farm magazines like *Farm Journal*, regional magazines like the *Missouri Ruralist*, and specialty magazines like the venerable Hoard's *Dairyman*. Magazine readership soared during the 1920s with reportedly 600 agriculture magazines on the market. But many became economic casualties of the Depression, and the number had dropped to around 200 by 1938, according to an article in *Scribner's* magazine (September 1938).

Many farm-equipment enthusiasts have found themselves buying technical manuals and old farm magazines. When most Americans lived on a farm, magazines provided most of the technical information and farm advice as well as entertainment. And the advertisements themselves provide a lot of information today about related products: feeds, seeds, pesticides, and manures. Most of these products and the companies that made them have disappeared, but old farm magazines are good, fairly available (and usually cheap) sources of technical information for old tractors and related machinery.

According to magazine historian James Wood, the oldest continuously published magazine in America is an agricultural journal. That distinction goes to the *Farm Journal*, a publication that started out nearly 120 years ago and was taken over by the Curtis Publishing Company around the beginning of the century. Founded in 1877 in one of the traditional American literary centers, Philadelphia, it had

Farm magazines like *The Furrow*, distributed only to John Deere customers, are collectible and very interesting. This magazine celebrated its 100th birthday in 1995, making it one of the oldest, continuously printed periodicals in America. *John Deere Archives*

more than 200,000 subscribers in the 1880s. In 1955 it absorbed the venerable publication *The Country Gentleman*, becoming America's largest farm magazine, with a circulation of over three million.

Successful Farming, founded in Des Moines, Iowa, in 1902 by former U.S. Senator Edwin T. Meredith, was a practical magazine that quickly had an enormous circulation. Currently published in several regional editions, its combined circulation is over one million copies. When Meredith retired as the head of the U.S. Department of Agriculture in 1922, he developed a companion magazine, *Better Homes and Gardens*. It also maintains an enormous circulation.

Some extremely interesting technical farm magazines have been out of print for decades, but they are still widely sought by collectors. Two magazines were printed just for threshermen: *The American Thresherman*, published from 1898 to 1932 in Madison, Wisconsin; and the *Thresherman's Review*, 1892 to 1928, originating in Detroit, Michigan.

Pacific Rural Press masthead, 1887.

Progressive Farming, founded in 1886, is a periodical aimed chiefly at southern farmers, but with a circulation of over a million, it is a force to be reckoned with.

Capper's was an interesting and influential regional periodical, born in Atchison, Kansas. Arthur Capper acquired the *Missouri Valley Farmer*, moved it to Topeka, Kansas, changed its name and developed its circulation. With its companion magazine, *Capper's Weekly*, a news magazine, it acquired a strong readership in agricultural mid-America. In addition, Capper acquired a number of other farm magazines, including the *Ohio Farmer*, the *Michigan Farmer*, and the *Pennsylvania Farmer*; eight magazines and a newspaper in all made up Capper's corporation. The little publishing empire helped him win a seat in Congress, where Senator Capper watched out for farm interests until his death in 1951. The Capper Magazine group was sold in 1956.

Farm and Fireside was first established by implement dealer Phineas T. Mast in 1877 as a way to merchandise his equipment. It was acquired by its editor, John Crowell, when millionaire Mast finally

passed away in 1898. The Crowell Publishing Company in Springfield, Ohio, also published *Collier's* and the *Woman's Home Companion*, but *Farm and Fireside* was the farmer's bible and it had 600,000 subscribers in 1915. Readership slumped and it was reorganized just at the beginning of the Depression. It found new life as the *Country Home*, a magazine slanted for farm readers.

Older editions of two of the most important American farm periodicals are still collected and read for their content and history. *The Country Gentleman* has the oldest bloodlines of any of the magazines, and it is notable for its technical information as well as its illustrations. It traces its heritage to The *Genessee Farmer*, first started in 1831, which was merged with *The Cultivator* in 1839. Merging again in 1866 with another weekly, it became known as the *Cultivator and Country Gentleman*.

The Cultivator and Country Gentleman was enormously popular, with a circulation of over a quarter-million before the Civil War in 1860. Circulation soared even more in the late nineteenth century. The magazine shortened its name to *The*

Country Gentleman and was still a major editorial force at the turn of the century. In 1911, *The Country Gentleman* was acquired by the Curtis Publishing Company, owners of *The Saturday Evening Post*. It was later acquired by another Philadelphia publication, the *Farm Journal*, in 1955.

The second periodical is newer but extremely interesting and historically important for entirely different reasons. The *Farmer's Wife* was an important magazine for farm women across the Upper Midwest. It was published exclusively for farm women by Dr. Ella Webb in St. Paul, Minnesota, and had a circulation of over a million subscribers during the 1920s and 1930s. It was eventually taken over by the Philadelphia-based *Farm Journal* magazine in 1939. It then appeared as an insert, a magazine within a magazine, after that date.

The *Farmer's Wife* offered solid information on child development and nutrition, bringing enormous help to relatively isolated farm wives in the days before auto ownership and telephones were widely available. In addition, the magazine developed farm women's clubs across middle America, clubs that were important groups that supported community betterment, higher standards for elementary education, and dozens of other civic improvements in rural areas.

Last, but not least, are the important farm periodicals that never appear in the librarians' lists but have had an enormous influence on American farming. Implement dealer Phineas P. Mast began *Farm and Fireside* magazine in order to sell his products. Other dealers and distributors took notice. One of the most collectible magazines today is called *The Furrow*, now published by the John Deere implement company for owners of John Deere tractors. When you bought a Deere tractor, your name was entered onto the subscription list for *The Furrow*. Since these farm magazines were not publicly subscribed, they do not usually appear in libraries, but they do show up frequently in farm sales and swap meets. They are an important source of information about farm equipment and implements, despite the obvious commercial bias.

Information for Collectors

One of the most authoritative sources for information about old magazines, including early farm journals, is a five-volume reference book found in many libraries called *A History of American Magazines* by Frank Luther Mott. Published by the Harvard University Press starting about 1938, this series is sensible and readable. It is considered to be the basic reference about American periodicals.

Old magazines, manuals, and farm books are frequently fragile and need special handling. A good rule of thumb is to give your books and magazines the same care you would give yourself: Don't sit in the sun and don't get overheated, damp, or dusty. Lying in the corner under various storage boxes isn't good for you, and it's not good for your collectible periodicals, either. Put them inside a dust cover to protect them. The archival sleeves sold by many stationery stores are the best protection for them. But if that is not possible, just put them inside a paper bag, away from direct light and heat, to keep them from deteriorating.

In addition to the general farm periodicals, there were dozens of farm magazines devoted to specialty farming. There were magazines for poultrymen, millers, dairymen . . . the list goes on. These are especially collectible not only because there were fewer of them printed, but because they are frequently a wonderful source of information about the vitality of a particular agricultural industry.

Important Events in American Farm History

1842   The first grain elevator is constructed in Buffalo, New York.

1853   Luther Tucker introduces *The Country Gentleman* magazine.

1855   Michigan Agricultural College is established.

1856   Condensed milk is developed and patented by Gail Borden. Food preservation and processing is now a commercial operation.

1862   The American Civil War begins, and some of the most important pieces of legislation ever to affect farming and rural life are passed. President Lincoln signs the Homestead Act, establishing homesteads of 160 acres for individuals who will stay on the land for five years. The Railroad Finance Act allows the railroad to own land on either side of the railroads. The railroad then delivers hundreds of European immigrant farmers to America. President Lincoln approves the Morrill Act, providing for the establishment of land-grant colleges. This act sets aside 30,000 acres in each state for every member sent to Congress. The United States Department of Agriculture is created by Congress. There are 18 branches, which are variously designed to help the farmer by doing everything from collecting weather data to researching soil conditions.

1867   The National Grange is established. A fraternal farm organization, it is sometimes known as the Patrons of Husbandry.

1869   The Golden Spike is set in a silver rail. Railroads east and west are joined and farmers can ship their products across country. This increased competition results in an economic depression. James Oliver patents his chilled plow.

1871   The first Grange laws regulating the railroads are passed in Illinois.

1873   The first silo is constructed.

1874   The patent on barbed wire is issued to Joseph Glidden of Dekalb, Illinois. Osage orange tree seed prices plummet.

1877   *Farm and Fireside* magazine is founded by Phineas P. Mast as the house organ for his implement-manufacturing company.

1879   Congress passes legislation for second-class mail, providing low-cost postage for periodicals.

1882   The modern cream separator is introduced to America from Sweden.

1885   Killing cold hits cattle ranchers.

1886   Record blizzards hurt farmers.

1887   The Hatch Act provides $15,000 annually to each state for agricultural research and experimentation.

1897   Curtis buys *The Saturday Evening Post* and two years later a new editor, George Lorimer, begins editing for popular tastes. Curtis also acquires the venerable publication *The Country Gentleman,* transforming it as well.

1903 Charles Hart and Charles Parr begin the manufacture of gasoline tractors in Charles City, Iowa. Congress adds the parcel-post system to the post office.

1913 The name 4-H (Head, Heart, Hand, Health) is adopted by service clubs for farm youth. The clubs originated in Illinois.

1914 World War I begins. American farmers are asked to help feed Europe. This brings prosperity to many American farmers.

1916 Congress passes the Federal Farm Loan Act, which establishes the federal farm loan system with its twelve regional banks. Congress also passes the Federal Road Act with the stated objective of aiding the construction of toll-free roads that would allow the farmer to bring resources to market.

1922 *Better Homes and Gardens* magazine is started in Des Moines, Iowa; it has a circulation

The Country Gentleman
Loring A. Schuler, Editor

JANUARY, 1927

The Country Gentleman masthead, 1927.

of over one million by 1928.

1925 Rural Free Delivery is implemented.

1929 The Rural Electrification Act funds electric power to farms.

1933 The Agricultural Adjustment Act establishes subsidies for farm products. The economic Depression of the 1930s coupled with the drought in the Dust Bowl and locust infestations cause impoverishment for many farmers. The Federal Farm Credit Act of 1933 modifies and somewhat replaces the Loan Act of 1916.

1935 Rural Electrification Administration established by President Roosevelt.

1939 The war begins in Europe, and Americans prepare to feed their allies.

1941 America enters World War II and farmers are asked to increase production.

1949 A rural telephone program is started by the Rural Electrification Association.

Recommended Reading

Books about Farm History

Boorstin, Daniel J. *The Americans: The Democratic Experience.* New York: Random House, 1973.

Fite, Gilbert C. *The Farmer's Frontier 1865–1900.* Norman, Oklahoma; London: University of Oklahoma Press, 1966.

Jones, Bryan. *The Farming Game.* Lincoln: University of Nebraska Press, 1982.

Rasmussen, Wayne D., ed. *Readings in the History of American Agriculture.* Urbana: University of Illinois Press, 1960.

Collectible Texts and Handbooks about Farming

Gardner, Charles M. *The Grange—Friend of the Farmer 1867–1947.* Washington, D.C.: The National Grange, 1949.

Lewis, Lloyd. *Wright, John S.: Prophet of the Prairies.* Chicago: The Prairie Farmer Publishing Company, 1941.

Seymour, E. L. D., B.S.A., ed. *Farm Knowledge—Farm Management.* New York: Prepared Exclusively for Sears Roebuck and Co. Doubleday, Farrar, & Co., 1918.